Praise for *Holy Noticing*

Ancient wisdom and current research converge in a most helpful guide. You can't afford to lose your mind!

JOHN ORTBERG, senior pastor of Menlo Church, and author of *Eternity Is Now in Session*

A few years ago, a leader challenged me with the idea that great leaders are a "non-anxious presence." That idea awakened me to how anxious, hurried, and unaware I was. Charles Stone's new book, *Holy Noticing*, provides a pathway for understanding the concept of mindfulness from a biblical perspective and equips you to thrive in an exhausting world. An amazing resource!

JENNI CATRON, leadership coach and founder of The 4Sight Group

In *Holy Noticing*, Charles offers an amazing array of unique ways to connect deeply with God and discover your purpose in the world. Grounded in Scripture, rooted in church history, and immensely practical, this book might well become a trusted guidebook for your spiritual journey.

TRICIA MCCARY RHODES, affiliate professor, Fuller Seminary and author of several books on spiritual formation, including *The Soul at Rest*

God has given us a capacity to be attentive, mindful, to notice—when this is done with a holy purpose, we can be transformed into the likeness of Christ. Charles Stone's new book, *Holy Noticing*, is a brilliant blend of theological wisdom, psychological truth, and personal experience laying out such a path of transformed living. I will be recommending this book wherever I go.

SHAUN LAMBERT, Baptist minister, counsellor, author, and mindfulness researcher

Holy Noticing combines the principles of cognitive neuroscience with the practices of nearly every Christian tradition to help us learn a profound shalom. Dr. Stone meticulously distinguishes trendy types of mindfulness from historical Christian approaches to living each moment in the presence of Jesus. Stone methodically teaches practical ways to learn shalom that can endure suffering and difficulties. Being present when life happens opens the way to find Jesus with us and bring balance to our minds. While the book provides excellent information, documentation, and instruction, the benefits go to those who will faithfully practice what they have read.

E. JAMES WILDER, neurotheologian and Life Model theoretician at Life Model Works, international speaker, and coauthor of *Rare Leadership*

Holy Noticing is a book where Scripture meets neuroscience meets spiritual disciplines. Charles's writing is biblically grounded and practically helpful. I am already putting these principles into practice. In this world of incessant distraction, constant noise, and sound-bite attention spans, we must learn the art of *Holy Noticing*.

LANCE WITT, founder of Replenish Ministries

Dr. Charles Stone is a prominent thought leader in the world of professional coaching with regard to brain science. Coupled with his theological training and experience as a pastor, he is uniquely qualified to address the powerful spiritual discipline of Christian mindfulness. *Holy Noticing* is a ground-breaking book examining the intersections of our mind, will, and emotions with our spirit and with God.

CHRISTOPHER MCCLUSKEY, president of *Professional Christian Coaching Institute; cohost of Professional Christian Coaching Today*

I received an advance read of Charles's new book at just the right time. I'm in one of the busiest seasons of my life and was beginning to feel the weight of stress on my soul. I needed the encouragement to slow down and do some *Holy Noticing*.

RON EDMONDSON, CEO, Leadership Network

Dr. Charles Stone's new book, *Holy Noticing*, is a gift to Christian leaders. Charles has always been a trusted resource for me in determining my unique makeup as a person and then leveraging that for God's glory and the expansion of His kingdom. We know that as a man thinks in his heart, so is he. Therefore, few things are as important as renewing your mind and simply thinking right. This book will help you. Get it today!

BRIAN DODD, director of New Ministry Partnerships, INJOY Stewardship Solutions

HOLY
NOTICING

© 2019 by
CHARLES STONE

All rights reserved. No part of this book may be reproduced in any form without permission in writing from the publisher, except in the case of brief quotations embodied in critical articles or reviews.

All Scripture quotations, unless otherwise indicated, are taken from the Holy Bible, New International Version®, NIV®. Copyright © 1973, 1978, 1984, 2011 by Biblica, Inc.™ Used by permission of Zondervan. All rights reserved worldwide. www.zondervan.com. The "NIV" and "New International Version" are trademarks registered in the United States Patent and Trademark Office by Biblica, Inc.™

Scripture quotations marked ESV are from the ESV® Bible (The Holy Bible, English Standard Version®), copyright © 2001 by Crossway, a publishing ministry of Good News Publishers. Used by permission. All rights reserved.

Scripture quotations marked MSG are taken from THE MESSAGE. Copyright © by Eugene H. Peterson 1993, 1994, 1995, 1996, 2000, 2001, 2002. Used by permission of NavPress Publishing Group.

Scripture quotations marked NLT are taken from the Holy Bible, New Living Translation, copyright ©1996, 2004, 2015 by Tyndale House Foundation. Used by permission of Tyndale House Publishers, Inc., Carol Stream, Illinois 60188. All rights reserved.

All emphasis in Scripture has been added.

Published in association with the literary agency of The Steve Laube Agency, 24 W. Camelback Rd. A635, Phoenix, AZ 85013

Edited by Connor Sterchi
Interior design: Ragont Design
Cover design: Erik M. Peterson
Cover image of human brain copyright © 2018 by maglyvi/Shutterstock (157155017). All rights reserved.

ISBN-13: 978-0-8024-1857-9

We hope you enjoy this book from Moody Publishers. Our goal is to provide high-quality, thought-provoking books and products that connect truth to your real needs and challenges. For more information on other books and products written and produced from a biblical perspective, go to www.moodypublishers.com or write to:

Moody Publishers
820 N. LaSalle Boulevard
Chicago, IL 60610

1 3 5 7 9 10 8 6 4 2

Printed in the United States of America

I lovingly dedicate this book to my wonderful wife, Sherryl, who has stood by my side in ministry and in life for almost 40 years. She exudes the spirit of a true "holy noticer."

Contents

The Spiritual and Practical Benefits of Holy Noticing

*What is mankind that you are mindful of them,
human beings that you care for them?*
—PSALM 8:4

A mindful person relishes wisdom.
—PROVERBS 10:23 MSG

AS I FUMBLED WITH MY KEYS to open the door, I heard the phone ring inside. I finally opened the door, ran into the kitchen, and picked up the receiver. I hadn't expected him to call so quickly. I listened as he explained.

It was a call no parent should ever have to endure.

Although he tried to temper the news, I heard little else after he revealed it. As if an invisible hand were squeezing my lungs, I couldn't breathe. My heart throbbed. My face flushed. My hands shook. Nausea rose in my throat. The dingy yellow paint on the kitchen wall began to blur as tears pooled in my eyes. He said they'd call soon to arrange the emergency surgery.

I placed the receiver in its cradle and steadied myself against the kitchen counter. I took a deep breath and smelled the scent of that morning's slightly burned breakfast toast. I tried to compose myself before I walked into the den. I sat down next to her on the carrot-colored carpet and cradled her tiny body in my arms. She was oblivious to what awaited her. I rocked her back and forth, back and forth, back and forth as salty tears streamed down my face. In my mind I kept thinking . . .

Little one-year-old girls aren't supposed to get brain tumors.
Little one-year-old girls aren't supposed to get brain tumors.
Little one-year-old girls aren't supposed to get brain tumors.
Yet I could not deny reality.

For the next twenty seven years, my wife and I fought and fought and fought against that despicable intrusion.

That all-consuming fight to save my youngest daughter's life led me to discover a lost spiritual art: noticing things with a holy purpose. It's what King David wrote about in Psalm 8:4 when he marveled at how God was mindful of man.

It awakened my soul and changed my life.

This book tells of that awakening.

What If?

Our journey with Tiffany made me think more often about what matters most in life. And as I began to discover this ancient biblical practice, I asked myself this seemingly odd question: *What if I could add a full month to my life this year?*

Would I?

Would you?

I don't mean calendar time, that you could morph twelve months into thirteen. However, I do mean quality time—doing more of what really matters to you—a month more each year. The apostle Paul refers to this when he admonishes us to "mak[e] the most of every opportunity" (Eph. 5:16).

What if . . .

. . . you rushed less?

. . . you engaged life at a deeper level?

. . . you reduced anxiety and fear in your life?

. . . you ran less on autopilot and lived with greater awareness?

. . . you could read the Bible and pray without your mind constantly wandering?

. . . you were more present for your kids, your spouse, your friends, yourself, God?

. . . you could recall the past or think about the future while not being imprisoned by either or wishing for a better moment?[1]

. . . you lived more in the present moment, enjoying it for what it is, rather than ruminating over past regrets, misconstruing and misreading what people think about you in the present, or speculating or worrying about the future?

What if you could do these? Would you?

Most of us live distracted lives. We want to get to a next better moment but then fail to notice the present one. We lack space between one task and the next, one thought and the next, one more email and the next.

Most of us live distracted lives. We want to get to a next better moment and fail to notice the present one.

I'm guilty of that very thing.

Social media, TV, work deadlines, and family stress easily rob our joy in the present and curb our engagement in the moment. In fact, experts say that we only fully live in the present moment, enjoying its blessings, two waking hours each day.[2] And rehashing and rehearsing negative experiences, depending on their severity, can stick with us for hours or days. The result? Poor decision-making, stress, relationship tension, a lackluster spiritual life, a boring devotional life, and misery.

Yet if you reclaimed just *two hours* every day, you would gain an extra month *every single year* to truly live life; to flourish; to create enough space to engage, notice, and appreciate what's truly important.

To personalize this, what if . . .

. . . you sensed your teenage daughter's tinge of sadness after school one day and that led to a heart-connecting conversation?

. . . you paused to notice fresh buds on your long dormant chrysanthemum and your joy for gardening was rekindled?

. . . you stopped to listen to your wife's struggle rather than trying to fix it, or her, which led to a deepened bonding with her?

. . . you prayed with deeper fervor for your wayward child because your mind wandered less?

. . . you stilled your soul to sense the Spirit's gentle nudge to call a distant friend?

Is that possible?

Could that really happen?

Yes it can.

Scripture, church history, and neuroscience show us how. It's what I call *holy noticing,* being fully present and mindful in each moment God has given us. I've defined *mindfulness* in this book as *the art of holy noticing—noticing, with a holy purpose, God and His handiwork, our relationships, and our inner world of thoughts and feelings.*

The Mindful Way

Mindfulness is a big deal in today's culture. Businesses such as Apple, sports figures such as basketball player Kobe Bryant, and the popular press such as *Time* magazine have all given it their stamp of approval. Governments are spending hundreds of millions of dollars researching it,[3] and it has become a billion-dollar-a-year business.[4] In fact, Apple chose a mindfulness app as their app of the year for 2017.[5]

But should Christians embrace it just because everyone else is doing it? No. Much about mindfulness in popular culture has nothing to do with God, Jesus, the Bible, or Christianity. And "Christianizing" the latest fad dilutes the faith and can lead us astray.

However, does God's Word support, and does Christian history illustrate, Christians using some of these techniques as tools for spiritual growth?[6] Yes. It's a lost spiritual discipline that believers should reclaim.

J. I. Packer writes that this kind of practice is

a lost art today, and Christian people suffer grievously from their ignorance of the practice.

Meditation is the activity of calling to mind, and thinking over, and dwelling on, and applying to oneself, the various things that one knows about the works and ways and purposes and promises of God. It is an activity of holy thought, consciously performed in the presence of God, under the eye of God, by the help of God, as a means of communion with God.[7]

And in a TV interview a few years before his death, Billy Graham was asked what he would do over if he could do things differently. In his inimitable way, he said, "I'd spend more time in meditation and prayer."[8]

Holy noticing is an ancient Christian practice that helps us flourish spiritually and engage the present moment to pause and notice what is happening *now*, all with a holy purpose. The Hebrew word *shalom* illustrates spiritually flourishing.

Shalom was a word often used by the Hebrew people as a greeting and a farewell. While usually translated "peace," it actually describes something much more profound. It implies completeness, soundness, wholeness, and experiential peace. The prophet Isaiah used a double "shalom, shalom" in Hebrew in Isaiah 26:3, which the NIV translates as "perfect peace." Essentially *shalom* describes a fully awakened soul engaged in the present moment, which holy noticing helps us experience.

> Mary was fully present in the moment for Jesus, something we often fail to do.

Perhaps this is what Mary experienced as she sat at the feet of Jesus, while her sister fretted about lunch (see Luke 10:38–42). Mary was fully present in the moment for Jesus, something we often fail to do.

This quote from an unknown source, although often attributed to a Nazi war camp survivor, captures what Mary did in her encounter with Jesus: "Between stimulus and response, there is a space. In that space lies our freedom and our power to choose our response. In our response lies our growth and our happiness."[9]

This space, between stimulus and response, is a crucial window into real peace, *shalom*, human flourishing, full engagement in the present moment, noticing with a holy purpose. The wider the space in time, the greater the opportunity for *shalom*. Holy noticing helps expand that space between stimulus and response giving us "the opportunity to think and feel differently, which give the freedom to choose the best way to solve problems."[10] It frees us from the gravitational pull toward unpleasant and difficult thoughts and emotions.

Neuroscientists have discovered that how well we regulate our internal responses (thoughts and emotions) and external responses (body language, words, displays of emotion) is essential to our well-being.[11] By growing this *space* through this practice, the Holy Spirit can help us control more consistently our emotions, thoughts, and how we display them to others. This in turn enhances our relationship with Jesus, others, and even ourselves.

Mindful versus Mindless

Unfortunately, we often don't live in the moment, in this *space*. Rather than being mind*ful*, we often become mind*less*. We flit from one distraction to another, trying to satisfy our every whim.[12] When we live mindlessly, we entangle ourselves in unhealthy thoughts and afflictive emotions. We crucify ourselves between two crosses. One rehashes and replays difficulties from the past that we cannot change. The other rehearses and ruminates over problems that *might* occur in the future that we cannot control.

As a result, we seldom joyfully and fully engage the present moment. Holy noticing makes us become more aware of our internal world as we respond to stimuli from our outer world. It helps us expand that space between a stimulus and our internal or external response. When we do that, God's Spirit empowers us to live more fully in the moment in a nonreactionary and nonjudgmental way. We're able to step off the treadmill of the past, stop anxiously replaying what might happen in the future, and engage the present with joy and peace, *shalom*.

As a spiritual skill, this way of life involves three ways of *looking*: (1) looking in (at our thoughts, body states, and emotions), (2) looking out (at our relationships and our immediate environment), and (3) looking up (at our relationship with Jesus). We might even call this, "mind*Full*ness" because "our being is filled with the presence of God."[13]

Support from Scripture and Church History

Living a mindful life has a rich Christian tradition that stretches back over the last two thousand years.[14] Although at times some who have practiced it have taken a few weird theological turns, it's been used by believers to still and quiet their hearts;[15] be more fully present to God in the moment;[16] bring their thoughts back to Jesus;[17] and cultivate a present-moment awareness of God's purpose, presence, and love.[18]

Fundamentally, it teaches us to mentally and physically pause. This pause helps us engage the present moment, experiencing what God has given us at *that* moment as we pay attention to our inner and outer world and to our responses to both. It helps us take notice of important concerns that we might otherwise unconsciously avoid: our body states, emotions, thoughts, and attention itself. By doing so, we develop the ability to focus on what's most important: God and people. It's a God-given capacity that we can develop to help us pay attention, be aware, and fully engage. As a spiritual practice, it helps us notice things, with a holy purpose.

Jesus clearly modeled and embodied this way of life.[19] We see it in these ways as one author wrote:

> His stillness and dignity in the face of humiliation and suffering; his lack of defensiveness in response to aggressive questioning; his full attentiveness to the people who come to him for help, even in the midst of the hustle and bustle of a demanding crowd; his alertness to the subtlety of the devil's temptations; and yet his honesty and awareness of his own fear in Gethsemane and his experience of abandonment on the cross.[20]

Many scriptural accounts reflect how Jesus lived in the present moment.

- Although thirsty Himself, He quenched the thirsty heart of a woman at a well (John 4:7–15).

- Although pressed by crowds, He knew that a sick woman had in desperation touched His robe for healing (Mark 5:24–34).

- Although His disciples tried to inhibit Him, He welcomed little children into His arms (Mark 10:13–16).

- Although demands mounted, He spent leisure time with Mary and Martha (Luke 10:38–42).

- Although tempted by Satan in the desert, thoughts, and feelings about power and wealth didn't preoccupy His mind (Matt. 4:1–11).

- Although a hectic schedule loomed, He stopped to pay attention to cries from lepers (Luke 17:11–14).

- And although He had only three years of public ministry, He often withdrew from the crowds to spend time alone with His Father (Mark 1:35; Luke 5:16).

One stand-out episode in Jesus' life illustrates this, which I already alluded to above. During His visit with Mary and Martha, He contrasted their responses to His presence with them. He drew attention to Mary's present-moment engagement with Him and lovingly admonished Martha for her busyness. And a different Mary, Mary Magdalene, the first to arrive at the empty tomb after Jesus' resurrection, shows how we can miss being in the moment (see John 20). Her grief kept her from initially noticing the risen Christ.

We might also parallel holy noticing to the role John the Baptist played in the life of Jesus. John paved the way for the coming Messiah so that the people would be ready to receive Him when that moment arrived. Although it doesn't necessarily fix difficulties in our lives, holy noticing helps prepare us by opening up a space where those difficulties might be fixed, if need be. It takes a further step by showing us that sometimes we need not "fix" things. The "fix" can often come through simple awareness. It teaches us "the skill of opening things up—bringing concerns to the surface—so that, in God's time and in God's way, they might be healed or restored (Mark 4:22)."[21]

Finally, Jesus captured the essence of this practice in His rebuke of Peter in Mark 8:33: "'Get behind me, Satan!' he said. 'You do not have in mind the concerns of God, but merely human concerns.'" As we hone our ability to be present in the moment of moral choosing, we will more consistently choose the "concerns of God" rather than "the human concerns" that vie for our attention. As holy noticing becomes an ongoing trait in our lives—as a skill we can learn—it will profoundly benefit our lives, our relationship with God, and those around us.

My Personal Struggles

I've been a committed Christian for almost five decades. I've served Jesus vocationally as a pastor for almost four decades. I've read, studied, and memorized the Bible. I've practiced spiritual disciplines. Yet something was amiss. My neatly packed theology—love God, do the right spiritual things, and peace will result—wasn't working. It was like Morpheus in *The Matrix* when he said, "You don't know what it is, but it's there, like a splinter in your mind, driving you mad." I wondered, *Do I have a splinter in my mind?*

At times I could not stop the incessant mental chatter about such issues as an ongoing conflict with a church leader, uncertainty about our church's financial future, or discouragement that my church was not growing. As I lay in bed at night, unable to sleep, I prayed. I quoted Scripture. I commanded Satan to leave me alone. I took melatonin. I ate Cheetos. But whatever I did to quiet my mind failed. When I tried to force my mind to *not* think about these issues, my mind became like a megaphone, amplifying those thoughts and emotions.

Has that ever happened to you? You try not to worry. You tell yourself to stop being anxious. You try every spiritual trick you know and nothing seems to work. Finally you drift off to sleep—at 1:00 a.m. And at 4:00 a.m. you wake up and the same nagging issues immediately bombard your mind. In my journey learning about holy noticing, I realized I was not alone in my struggles, as one author delightfully captured in a poem. In it he says if you can be calm in difficulty, not envy others, fall asleep easily, and be content no matter what, you're probably a dog.[22]

As I sought answers, I began to read everything I could on social cognitive neuroscience, the science that examines how neural activity influences social relationships, emotions, and mental processes. My engineering degree had given me a strong science background, and my two ministry degrees had given me a strong biblical worldview. I wondered if the missing piece for me, however, lay in intersecting brain insight with biblical truth.

My journey led me to enroll in an executive master's degree program in the neuroscience of leadership. To earn my degree, I wrote my final paper on mindfulness and based it on my review of hundreds of scientific papers on the subject. It also led me to write a book on brain insight and Christian leadership—*Brain-Savvy Leaders: The Science of Significant Ministry*. This journey led me to discover this lost art of holy noticing.

When I began to study it, I initially felt uncomfortable with the practice. I tend to be more cerebral—think a version of Mr. Spock in the original TV show *Star Trek*, without the ears but with the same sized nose. The emotional side of spirituality has always felt a bit uncomfortable. As I began to read widely on the subject, however, several wise Christian authors, including Tim Keller, helped soften me toward the emotional side of spirituality, a significant area that holy noticing addresses. He quoted a theologian that impacted his view of the emotional side of spirituality when he wrote,

The assurance of secure love in God is "mystical in the best sense of the word." . . . We must not "underemphasize the emotional ground" of experience. "Some veer away from this idea because of its subjectivity, but the abuse of the subjective in some circles cannot exclude the 'mystical' and emotional dimensions of Christian experience."[23]

As I continued to learn more about it and began to incorporate the practice into my spiritual disciplines, I began to experience greater peace. I slept better (far less Cheetos). I felt better physically. I reacted less. I was more present and engaged with others in their pain. My relationships improved. I controlled my thoughts better. I became more comfortable in my own skin. My spiritual life moved to a new level. My soul seemed more alive and awakened to others and to Jesus. It was helping me experience what Jesus promised in John 10:10, when He said, "I have come that they may have life, and have it to the full."

Although from time to time I still struggle with anxious emotions and thoughts, the splinter in my mind seems to be gone. I wish I had known twenty-five years ago what I share in this book.

The Benefits in Brief

Although throughout the book I detail many benefits of holy noticing, I want to touch on them here. This practice is certainly no panacea that solves every problem, but neuroscientific research continues to uncover more practical benefits. Evangelical theologians also agree that we must consider increasing neuroscientific knowledge because it "may yield important insights that can be integrated with a biblical and theological understanding of Christian meditation."[24]

And on a broader note about how science contributes to our faith, Mark Noll, world-renowned Christian historian, wrote these words:

> Coming to know Christ provides the most basic possible motive for pursuing the tasks of human learning. . . .
>
> if what we claim about Jesus Christ is true, then evangelicals should be among the most active, most serious, and most open-minded advocates of general human learning. Evangelical hesitation about scholarship in general or about pursuing learning wholeheartedly is, in other words, antithetical to the Christ-centered basis of evangelical faith.[25]

Christian psychologists have also found that we can benefit from a mindful life in areas such as encouraging deeper connection to God's heart of compassion, helping us turn toward things we avoid in ourselves and in the world around us, enhancing Bible reading, and growing our character and wisdom.[26]

Holy noticing also benefits our brains. One researcher wrote that this practice "may be a powerful way to affect *neuroplasticity*—the brain's ability to form new connections in response to the environment—as well as *epigenetics*, the regulation of genes (turning on and off their expression) in response to the environment."[27] So, as science continues to discover our brain's malleability, holy noticing can literally "rewire" our brains for the good.

It's important to remember that a mindful life is not all about me and my happiness. Ultimately, it's a spiritual discipline that leads us right into the heart of Jesus' teaching and example of how to live a spiritual life.[28] It's not a magical elixir for every emotional or mental distress. Yet, as you learn the art of holy noticing, you will spiritually flourish, notice things with a holy purpose, stay engaged in the present moment with greater joy, and connect more deeply to Jesus and others.

So, what about that phone call? What happened to our youngest daughter?

That phone call decades ago launched my journey of discovery into holy noticing.

Bonus material available at www.holynoticing.com/bonus:

• Printable definition of Christian mindfulness

• Placard-sized printable quote of "Between stimulus and response, there is a space."

PART 1

NOTICING WITH
A HOLY PURPOSE

CHAPTER 1

What Mindfulness Is, What It's Not, and Why It Matters

Mindfulness in the Christian vision is to
"let that same mind be in [us] that was in Christ Jesus."
—STEFAN GILLOW REYNOLDS

In silence and in meditation on the eternal truths, I hear the
voice of God which excites our hearts to greater love.
—C. S. LEWIS

THE STORY ACTUALLY STARTED a few weeks prior to that phone call. My youngest daughter, Tiffany, was a year old at the time. It was Christmas morning, and as she sat in her highchair, I fed her pureed apple sauce. While cajoling her to eat, I noticed that her left eye quivered like Jell-O. My anxiety spiked and I showed my wife. Whatever Christmas cheer we felt was quickly dashed. Within a week we arranged an emergency appointment with a pediatric neurologist who assured us it was nothing to worry about. He ordered a routine CT scan "just to be sure." That scan began our multidecade journey.

A few days later we took her to the hospital for the "routine" scan. After the scan we returned home, and as I was opening the front door, the phone rang. That's when I rushed inside, picked up the receiver, and heard the news.

The doctor said, "Mr. Stone, we discovered a lesion." I

thought, *A lesion . . . Certainly that's a simple problem that can be fixed with a simple solution.*

Then he clarified what a lesion was. I felt as though someone had stabbed me in the stomach when he said those words—words a parent should never have to hear: "Your daughter has a brain tumor."

Life would now take on new urgency as we would fight to save Tiffany's life. Within a short time, surgeons performed the first of more than ten brain surgeries she would eventually endure over the next twenty-nine years. She was hospitalized numerous times, received an experimental device implant in her brain, and had part of her brain surgically removed. However, after our long journey she is now doing quite well, and at the time of this writing, she is studying in seminary to become a hospital chaplain and counselor. My decades-long experience spurred me to pursue how our brains and mindfulness might intersect to influence our spiritual growth.

During one of our many visits to the hospital in Chicago where she was receiving treatment (when she was in her twenties), I experienced secular mindfulness for the first time. As a parent, my stress intensified each time we made a trip there for another surgery. During this particular hospital stay, my wife noticed a blurb in the hospital's daily newsletter about a daily mindfulness class they offered.

I thought, *Wow. What perfect timing. I'll check it out.* So a few minutes before the class began, I took the elevator to the fifth floor. As I walked toward the classroom, next to a small sandwich shop, I immediately felt anxious. A fully glassed wall enclosed the classroom, and I couldn't see inside because the glass was glazed. I paused and thought, *I wonder what they are doing in there?*

I considered turning around and skipping the class. But I mustered my courage, walked to the door, and slowly inched it open to avoid any squeaks that would alert them to my presence. What I saw quadrupled my anxiety. I first noticed the absence of chairs in the room and the subdued lighting. Then I saw that everyone was sitting on the floor cross-legged in the lotus position. Their palms lay on their knees, and their thumbs and forefingers had formed the "OK" sign. As I paused, I heard them droning in low-voiced unison, "Yaaaa-du. Yaaaa-du. Waaaaa-du. Waaaaa-du. The toe bone's connected to the foot bone."

Okay. Maybe I didn't hear *Dry Bones* being sung. But I was freaked out by what I saw. I slowly closed the door, turned on my heels, and made a beeline to the sandwich shop, hoping no one saw my rapid exit.

I needed a drink, a strong one. A Diet Dr Pepper (and I don't even drink Dr Pepper).

That was my initial experience with a secular approach to mindfulness. And that's probably a similar image for many Christians when they think about mindfulness—sit on the floor in a weird pretzel pose, turn the lights down low, and hum, "Yaaaa-du. Yaaaa-du." Fortunately, that does not accurately portray what I'm talking about in this book—noticing with a holy purpose.

The Art of Holy Noticing

At the outset, it's important to remember that our ultimate goal is not to use mindfulness simply to make us feel better—because science has discovered that it does just that—but rather to make us more like Christ (see Rom. 8:29; Eph. 4:13; Gal. 4:19).

For example, in the last few decades, scientific research has discovered that exercise is good for you. Exercise is exercise, though. We don't split it into secular exercise and Christian exercise. It benefits Christians and non-Christians alike. However, a believer can take exercise a step beyond. We exercise not simply to feel better and keep our hearts healthy (and that's a fine motive) but fundamentally to honor God. Because Scripture says that our bodies are temples of the Holy Spirit, when we exercise, we do it for God's glory. Our bodies are gifts entrusted to us by the One who created us. We honor Him when we take care of our bodies. And with healthy bodies, we can serve Him better.

Holy noticing is similar to exercise, but so much more. Although it brings tangible benefits such as a healthier brain (which, again, is a fine motive), it ultimately helps us love God and love others better. And even though some practices may resemble secular mindfulness (like slow breathing), we don't throw the baby out with the bathwater by rejecting science-based practices that may benefit anyone. Essentially, God created our brains to respond to these mindful practices in several positive ways. Holy noticing quiets our brain's circuitry when bombarded by afflictive emotions, negative thinking, and reactivity and amplifies our brain's circuitry to help us more consistently apply living out the mind of Christ.[1]

As I explained in the introduction, my definition of Christian mindfulness is *the art of holy noticing—noticing, with a holy purpose, God and His handiwork, our relationships, and our inner world of thoughts and feelings.*

This spiritual discipline is an art (there isn't just one right way to do it) that involves noticing with a *holy purpose*. We don't notice *just* to notice. We don't notice *just* to benefit ourselves. We notice, however, with God's purposes and perspectives in mind. What we notice first and foremost is God Himself. That involves noticing His handiwork, what's happening in our relationships, and our inner world of thoughts and feelings.

> **God models this pattern of noticing because He Himself is a perfect noticer. Nothing in our lives is too small or insignificant for Him to notice.**

God models this pattern of noticing because He Himself is a perfect noticer. Nothing in our lives is too small or insignificant for Him to notice. He knows the number of hairs on our head (Matt. 10:30). He noticed the Hebrews groaning under Egyptian bondage (Ex. 2:25). He notices our pain, our joys, our heartaches, and our happiness. The psalmist writes, "You keep track of all my sorrows. You have collected all my tears in your bottle. You have recorded each one in your book" (Ps. 56:8 NLT). God's sovereign nature reminds us that He knows and notices everything about us. Jesus modeled holy noticing in the Sermon on the Mount when He directed His hearers' attention to birds and flowers that we often overlook in our worrisome lives (Matt. 6:25–34). He also used the phrase, "He who has ears to hear, let him hear" (Matt. 11:15; Mark 4:9 ESV), to challenge us to pay close attention, to notice, to listen. The writer of Proverbs even admonishes us to notice things as tiny as an ant (Prov. 6:6). Holy noticing is a way to bring intentional awareness in the present moment to what and who is around us and what we're doing, thinking, and feeling—all from God's perspective.

A practical way to learn and practice this mindful lifestyle is with the easy-to-remember acronym BREATHe. Each component of this model begins with one letter of this word. The last letter, *e*, is actually the most important aspect of holy noticing. It ties everything together.

Holy noticing—noticing with a holy, God-focused purpose—means noticing your

- **B**ody: being aware of your physical body states and sensations;

- **R**elationships: assessing the health of your relationships;

- **E**nvironment: taking notice of your current surroundings, including sights, sounds, smells, and God's creation;

- **A**fflictive emotions or **A**ffect (a general term for emotions): acknowledging how you're currently feeling;

- **T**houghts: being conscious of your current thoughts;

- **H**eart: paying attention to the state of your spiritual life and the Holy Spirit's whisperings or impressions on your heart; and, to tie it all together,

- **e**ngage: engaging the world like Christ, practicing holy noticing in the mundane, the everyday, the ordinary.

One helpful way to describe this "noticing" posture comes from two neuroscientists[2] who created the counseling approach called acceptance and commitment therapy (ACT). They explain that we can choose from three different

perspectives in our imme-
diate experience: participant, participant-observer,
and observer. We shift between these perspectives
during our waking hours
and none is necessarily better than the other.

> **Holy noticing is a way to bring intentional awareness in the present moment to what and who is around us and what we're doing, thinking, and feeling—all from God's perspective.**

They illustrate these
perspectives with an amusement-park roller coaster. As a participant, you'd be in the front car simply to experience the thrill
of the ride. You don't necessarily care about who's around you.
For you, it's all about the immediate experience.

Or, you take the participant-observer perspective by sitting in a middle car and noticing not only your experiences but
also the experiences and reactions of the other riders. What
they do might even influence what you do. A brave soul might
lift her arms, which might motivate you to do the same.

Finally, you could take the observer perspective by not getting on the ride at all. You simply stand on the ground below so
you can notice the larger context, all the aspects of the ride and
the riders, their screams, their laughter, the coaster's loops,
and so on. You can even see what the participants can't—the
death-defying loop just beyond the next turn.

Noticing is like being the observer on the ground. In
mindfulness, noticing is the art you can learn to observe your
body sensations, your relationship dynamics, the environment
you're in, your affect (positive and negative emotions), your
thoughts, and the state of your heart, without reacting to them.

In the pages ahead, you'll learn several important mindsets
or skills that will help you gain the most from this way of living.

It will take practice to make it a way of life, but over time you will begin to see discernable benefits. Several biblical attitudes form the basis of holy noticing.[3]

1. Avoid the temptation to judge every thought and emotion (and other people as well), and avoid trying to immediately change them, unless you immediately sense they are sinful (see Matt. 7:1–5).

2. Cultivate patience by avoiding the drivenness to move to a better moment. Try not to let the clock rule your heart (see Prov. 14:29).

3. Foster a beginner's mindset by approaching your emotions and thoughts with childlike faith, curiosity, and wonder (see Matt. 18:2–4).

4. Trust in God's goodness, timing, and providence since you don't know everything (see John 14:1).

5. Embrace a nonstriving, restful posture to enjoy the journey of life, be less driven, and live in and appreciate the current moment better. This does not mean be lazy or passive (see Ps. 46:10).

6. Nurture acceptance as you learn to submit to your experiences, trusting that God is at work in them (see Ex. 14:14). This does not mean enduring abuse, sin, or injustice with passive resignation.

7. Practice letting go of what you think you need or must have, realizing that you aren't at the mercy of your passions and desires. This doesn't mean detachment from reality or nihilism (see Prov. 16, 32, 25, 28).

What Holy Noticing Is Not

Just as I struggled with my preconceived notions about mindfulness, perhaps you have as well. Maybe you've had an experience similar to the one I had with the secular class in the hospital. Most websites show pictures of people sitting in pretzel poses on tiny cushions while they appear to hum unintelligible sounds. Holy noticing is nothing like that.

Much secular mindfulness is founded upon Buddhism. But I want to emphasize that holy noticing is not Buddhism in disguise. Major differences exist between Christianity and Buddhism, one of which is that Buddhism is essentially a godless faith. You can be a practicing Buddhist and an atheist at the same time. And when Buddhists practice secular mindfulness, they seek detachment from self or personal identity. A believer who learns the art of holy noticing, however, emphasizes the value of the self as a reflection of God's image, rooted in our identity in Christ.

Holy noticing is not a New Age practice in which you strive to empty your mind, stop thinking, and thus subject yourself to malevolent spiritual forces. It is learning to pay attention to all the streams of information coming at you every day. Rather than giving us empty minds, this spiritual discipline helps us become *more* aware of our mental and emotional experiences while also recognizing Christ's presence in the moment. We don't stop thinking when we practice mindful living. Rather we stop *to* think. Rather than thought*less*ness, we become thought-full and mind-full of God's truth, power, promises, and presence.

This way of life is also not a self-absorbed, positive-thinking experience all about me and my happiness. On the contrary, it's a practice that helps us love others who are in need in tangible

> **Holy noticing does not replace but rather complements other spiritual disciplines such as prayer, Bible reading, and Scripture meditation.**

ways[4] as we see in the story of the Good Samaritan (see Luke 10:25–37). It helps us see the needs right before our very eyes, not just what we want to see. It motivates us to take action.

Holy noticing does not replace but rather complements other spiritual disciplines such as prayer, Bible reading, and Scripture meditation. It's a way to make other disciplines richer, more effective, less boring, and more meaningful. As you practice holy noticing, you'll discover that intercession, praise, confession, and meditation on Scripture overlap and naturally flow in and out of the discipline. It will even enhance the discipline of Christian community as you learn to be more fully present with others. And over time it will help your mind wander less during your devotional practices. It has especially helped me slow down to more deeply reflect upon Scripture.

Finally, holy noticing is not a cop-out or a way to escape or deny reality or sinful attitudes. It may actually make you *more* sensitive to sin and injustice that you may have ignored previously. It will give you a clearer picture of reality—what you are actually thinking and feeling. It will increase your appreciation for God's creation and give you greater wisdom in your relationships so that you can be more Christlike in them.

Why Holy Noticing Matters

In the chapters on the BREATHe model, I share many practical benefits related to this practice. However, a mindful lifestyle should matter to Christians who want to grow and live the abundant life Jesus promises us. I have learned that when we cultivate the art of holy noticing, these broad benefits will result.

1. We avoid spiritual forgetfulness.

In the book of Psalms, the psalmist records what often happens to us in our walk with God: our mental chatter and the stories we tell ourselves often lead us to forget God, what He has done, and what He is doing, at least temporarily. Psalm 78:11 reminds us about this pattern: "They forgot what he had done, the wonders he had shown them."

When we ruminate over and regret the *past*, we forget His mercy (e.g. we worry about how we will pay this month's bills when God has consistenly provided for us in the past).

When we misread or misconstrue something in the *present* (e.g., we read something negative into a glance from our boss), we forget His grace.

When we speculate and become anxious about the *future*, we forget His sovereignty (e.g., we fret over a difficult conversation we must have with our boss next week, yet every time that has happened, God has given us strength).

And when we try to think our way out of unhappy thoughts, our unhappiness can actually intensify. Initial fleeting emotions of sadness, anger, regret, fear, or worry can turn into full-fledged depression or anxiety if we incessantly ruminate on them.

Holy noticing, however, can help us counter our tendency to spiritually forget God. It helps interrupt our thought stream, which often gets hooked on unhealthy regrets and ruminations about the past, misrepresentations about the present, and worries about the future. It helps us spiritually remember by calming the brain's fear centers while simultaneously engaging our thinking centers so that we can think more clearly and biblically. It helps us *come to our senses* like the younger son in the prodigal son story came to his (Luke 15:11–32). And the Psalms often illustrate that thoughtful reflective practices serve as an antidote to spiritual forgetting (see Pss. 78, 103, 106, 137).

In another biblical example, Luke records two disciples on the road to Emmaus, walking with Jesus, although they didn't recognize Him. They walked with Him all day as they recounted their gloomy narrative of the recent events surrounding His death. Yet toward the end of their conversation "their eyes were opened and they recognized him" (Luke 24:30–31). This story illustrates that although Jesus is with us all day, our ruminations about the past and anxiety about the future often obscure our conscious awareness of Him.

> Although Jesus is with us all day, our ruminations about the past and anxiety about the future often obscure our conscious awareness of Him.

We forget that He is with us.

The narrative we add to our thoughts and emotions clouds reality. Holy noticing helps us become more aware of Jesus' moment-by-moment presence with us through His Spirit. It keeps us from looking only at the surface of things (see 2 Cor. 10:7).

2. We enhance our mental and emotional health.

And why is this important for a believer? Because we are a unified body, soul, and spirit (1 Thess. 5:23). When things go awry in our souls, our whole being is affected.

Neuroscientists have discovered specific brain processes involved in this practice. Although I briefly list these processes here, I will explain them in more detail in future chapters. Holy noticing helps us

- keep negative emotions from running unchecked;[5]

- avoid wrong assumptions and incorrect thought patterns;[6]

- have a greater awareness of our internal body sensations,[7] which can cue unhealthy, unconscious thinking patterns;

- "think about our thinking," which makes us consciously aware of unhealthy and sinful thinking[8] (we might call this mental reflection that the apostle Paul wrote about in Philippians 4:8); and

- identify less with difficult emotions.[9] We don't let them define our true self.

As a result, this way of life helps us more consistently act upon truth because we have the *mind of Christ* (2 Cor. 10:5). We become less defensive and less likely to react as we exercise the fruit of the Spirit (Eph. 4:22–23). We think more biblically as we put into our working memory (also called short-term memory) more truth (Phil. 4:8). We become more present in the moment for God and others. And we ruminate less often over negative thoughts.

3. We increase our happiness by changing our interior landscape.

We are the product of both nature and nurture. That is,

we inherited certain genetic traits from our parents' genes (nature), and how they raised us also fashions who we are (nurture). For example, when I was a teen, I had bad acne. My dad had bad acne. My mom has a rib on her right side that sticks out a bit from the rest of her ribs. I got that same rib. My dad can figure out how to fix almost everything. I never got that gene. My wife will affirm that.

Just as we received certain physical traits from our parents, we also inherited some of their mental and emotional natures. I tend to struggle with anxiety more than most. My mom dealt with that as well. On the positive side, my dad likes to laugh. I got some of that nature from him. My kids remind me, though, that when people laugh at my jokes, they're often just being nice and giving me what they call a "courtesy laugh." I disagree. I believe my genetically based humor is so advanced that it lies beyond most people's comprehension. Most people just don't get how funny I really am. That was a joke if you missed it. Again, my advanced genetically endowed humor at work here.

So how much does genetics influence happiness (our sense of joy and well-being in life, even in difficulties)? Even though happiness research is still in its infancy, psychologist Sonja Lyubomirsky's research[10] indicates that 50 percent of individual differences in happiness are determined by genes, 10 percent by life circumstances, and 40 percent by our intentional activities. So, 40 percent gives us significant latitude in how we can shape our happiness with God's help. Holy noticing can help make a difference with that 40 percent.

One study of forty-one biotech workers[11] who were given mindfulness training illustrates its influence over our happiness. After their training, the workers' brain scans showed a dramatic increase of their left prefrontal cortex activation (the part of the brain behind the temple) to right-prefrontal cortex activation. Left prefrontal cortex activation in this study indicated greater vitality and well-being, indicators of happiness.

This research study infers that changing our interior landscape—our thoughts and emotions—can shift our levels of happiness. A mindful lifestyle enhances the brain's ability to rewire itself through experience, thoughts, and behavior. It's called neuroplasticity. That is, the brain is more like pliable putty than rigid porcelain. What we think about and do changes our brains. When mindfulness affects neuroplasticity, it's like an electrician running new wiring to bring a house up to code. In other words, even the aging adult brain can change and be "brought up to code."

It's worth noting that studies I refer to in this book illustrate only the pragmatic effects that *may* derive from mindfulness training. Science can take us only so far, however. Don't believe every mindfulness study on the internet that claims to have discovered some new, amazing benefit from it. Just because something is labeled as scientific does not mean it is true. Although I love science (I'm a geek), science does not transform us. God does through the power of the Holy Spirit. He is the ultimate change agent, not a practice that a scientist says is good for you.

We certainly must learn from science because all truth is God's truth. But ultimate truth lies with God and His Word. Evidence-based science may inform us, but it doesn't ultimately transform us. It may illustrate some practical benefit gained from holy noticing, but, again, it does not change us. God does.

4. We are able to live more as human beings *rather than human* doings.

God created us with incredible minds that allow us to solve intricate problems. But sometimes our problem-solving mode does not serve us well. When we face emotional pain and stressful thoughts, we try to solve these problems. *Why do I feel this way? Where did these thoughts and feelings come from? What can I do to make them go away?*

This problem-solving mode is called the *doing mode*. And modern society (and original sin) has conditioned us to default to the *doing mode*. The *doing mode* tricks us to believe that productivity, speed, and efficiency are ultimate goals in life. When we stay in our *doing mode*, it is like being on autopilot all the time. We act with little clear thinking.

> **Our biggest interior problems lie not in our emotions or thoughts but in our response to them.**

We often try to fix these difficult thoughts and emotions by overthinking and brooding (a form of being in the *doing mode*). And when we expend mental resources on worry and fear in the *doing mode*, we leave fewer mental resources to simply "be" in the present moment.

Emotions aren't things to be fixed. They simply reflect our feeling and physical states. They are not meant to be solved but to be felt, notwithstanding that they can point to sin in our lives or sometimes can be sin themselves, requiring confession. Holy noticing helps us switch from our problem-solving *doing mode* to the more reflective *being mode* by strengthening the areas in the brain that help us more easily shift from a *doing mode* to a *being mode*.

Our biggest interior problems lie not in our emotions or

thoughts but in our response to them. We can't push a reset button to make our difficult emotions instantly go away. We can, however, respond to them in a different way. Practicing holy noticing can help rezone our neural networks toward healthier thinking and feeling patterns.

The apostle Paul reminds us in 1 Corinthians 10:13 that we may not be able to stop a temptation to ruminate over unhappy memories or dwell on negative self-talk. But we can stop what happens next. We can refuse to act upon that temptation. He writes, "When you are tempted, he will also provide a way out so that you can endure it."

Our *being mode* gives us a new perspective that frees us from overthinking, mentally reacting, and allowing afflictive emotions or thoughts to snowball. In the *being mode* we actually stay closer to truth, which in turn frees us. Jesus said in John 8:32 that when we know the truth, it sets us free. Knowing the truth in Jesus and knowing the truth about the present moment does indeed set us free.

As some researchers have stated, "While in the 'being mode,' negative cognitive and emotion patterns may still occur, but they are experienced from a decentered perspective—as objects of awareness that rise and pass naturally, rather than as problems to be solved."[12] Holy noticing helps us step outside our experience rather than getting caught up in it. It gives us a different perspective through observing and perceiving our thoughts and emotions. We don't necessarily change them (of course sometimes we most certainly must if they are sinful), but we change how we relate to them.

I mentioned the story of Mary and Martha in the prior chapter. It bears repeating as it best illustrates the difference between a *doing mode* and a *being mode*. Martha illustrates our culture's entrapment with performance, what we might call a human *doing*. Mary illustrates God's desire for us to be present in the moment as human *beings*. Mary sat at the feet of Jesus, while Martha was in the kitchen fretting about preparing a meal for Jesus and fuming about Mary's lack of support. I'm not implying that we should become passive and lazy people caught up in our inner world with no drive to achieve. We all need some of Martha's qualities. She was goal-oriented and persistent, and she followed through on her plans. She simply failed to switch gears. A lifestyle of holy noticing helps us switch gears from a problem-solving *doing mode* to a presence *being mode* when we need to. And of course, as we submit to the Holy Spirit, He is always at work, no matter which mode we may be in. (If you want to evaluate your *doing* versus *being* mode, download the quiz at www.holynoticing.com/bonus.)

5. We develop a lifestyle of holy noticing.

Researchers have categorized mindfulness as either a *trait* (a lifestyle, habit, or disposition stable over time)[13] or a *state* (temporary and may be induced by our current situation). As you grow in your ability to make holy noticing more of a trait in your life, you will more often bring an awareness of God's presence to your mind, heart, and activities, a posture Paul describes as "pray[ing] without ceasing" (1 Thess. 5:17 esv).

Oswald Chambers illustrates this state versus trait idea when he writes about mountaintop experiences versus living in the valley. He says that we are made for living in the valleys of life, not in the mountaintop experiences, even though we may want to live there.[14] He writes, "It is in the valley that we have to live for the glory of God. We *see* His glory on the mountain, but we never *live* for His glory there."[15]

The mountaintops are moments in our devotional practices, or even special moments during the normal course of a day, when we sense God's deep peace and presence in a conversation with a friend, in the beauty of a flower, or in a verse that pops out at us as we read the Bible. It's a blessing to experience these glimpses of *shalom*. However, when we live out that peace in the valleys, we are experiencing the *trait* of holy noticing, an enduring quality that indicates Jesus is permanently changing our hearts.

So what does the Bible *really* say about holy noticing? And does church history provide examples of its practice? In the next chapter, we'll explore these questions and look at the biblical support for holy noticing.

Bonus material available at www.holynoticing.com/bonus:

• The Doing vs. the Being Mode Quiz

CHAPTER 2

How the Bible and Church History Support This Ancient Spiritual Discipline

Music is not in the notes, but in the silence between them.
—DEBUSSY

I have discovered that all the unhappiness of men arises from one single fact, that they are unable to stay quietly in their own chamber.
—BLAISE PASCAL

DISTRACTIONS IN LIFE ARE NOTHING NEW.

We've faced them since Adam and Eve. The forbidden fruit was the prototypical distraction that led to the fall. Martha's distraction with preparing a meal *for* Jesus rather than simply being *with* Jesus provides great Bible study and sermon material for a mindful lifestyle (see Luke 10:39–42).

Yet, it's easier said than done.

The Martha and Mary story contrasts the difference between mindfulness and its opposite—mind*less*ness. Martha illustrates our culture's entrapment with performance, resulting in human *doings*. Mary illustrates God's desire for us to be present in the moment as human *beings*. Mary mindfully sat at the feet of Jesus, while Martha missed the moment as her thoughts and emotions overtook being mindfully present to Jesus.

The story also contrasts a busy outer life with a calm inner life. In this passage, Martha was busy, organized, and focused, yet she was also self-righteous, stressed, and judgmental. Life sometimes requires that we act like Martha simply to get stuff done, minus the negative qualities, however. Yet those qualities should be subservient to an inner quiet soul, which is what holy noticing fosters.

This eye-opening experiment illustrates how distraction keeps us from being fully present in the moment.

It was a normal day in the Washington, DC, subway. Like most days, musicians would ply their trade, hoping that passengers would toss a few dollars into a jar or guitar case. On this day, an average-looking guy in a baseball cap and white T-shirt positioned himself next to a garbage can. He left open his violin case, hoping a few of those dollars would make their way there.

> **Sadly, adults too easily lose the wonder and curiosity that children model for us. Holy noticing seems to come more easily for them.**

Over the next forty-three minutes during rush hour, he performed six classical pieces as more than one thousand passengers walked by. This performer, however, wasn't the average street performer.

His name? Joshua Bell.

His credentials? A child prodigy and famous violinist, who days before had played before a sold-out concert in Boston where concertgoers had paid up to a hundred dollars a ticket.

His music? Bach's *Chaconne*, regarded as one of the most difficult to play on the violin.

His instrument? A $3.5 million Stradivarius.

The result? A hidden camera revealed that only seven people stopped to watch his performance for at least a minute. What's most striking about this experiment was not that the adults missed an amazing experience, but that every time a child wanted to stop and listen, the parents rushed them along.[1] Sadly, adults too easily lose the wonder and curiosity that children model for us. Holy noticing seems to come more easily for them.

Likewise, if Martha had had her way, Mary would have missed those holy moments with Jesus. Holy noticing is a lifestyle that helps us develop a posture that captures more of those God moments.

In this chapter, I reference several key passages of Scripture that support this perspective, and I illustrate how Christians through history have practiced it to deepen their relationship with Jesus.

Biblical Roots

The word *mindfulness* is an English translation of an ancient Indian word in the Pali language (*sati*), which means "attention," "remembering," and "awareness."[2] However, the Hebrew word for mindful, *zakar* ("think about," "to remember," "call to mind"[3]), actually predates the Pali language by several hundred years.

We can also trace the word back to the Old English word *gemyndful*, which meant "of good memory." The Old English also had a form, *myndig*, which meant "recollecting" or "thoughtful." It then passed into Middle English as *myndful*. In that form, it appeared in the King James Version in Psalm 8:4 ("What is man, that thou art mindful of him?"). As an

English word, it derives from the Latin word *memor*, meaning "memory." Yet in the Psalms, it means more than just to "remember," but to "put something into practice, specifically to show concern."[4]

The Bible repeatedly emphasizes the mind's role for a Christ follower. In the NIV translation, the word *mind(s)* appears more than 150 times. And mindfulness involves the thoughts that course through our minds and how we relate to them. Even the Greek word for "repentance," *metanoia*, means "change of *mind*." Kallistos Ware, scholar of Greek spirituality, calls metanoia "mental watchfulness with alertness to the present moment."[5] And the NIV includes more than 230 references to the word *remember*, and eighteen references to the word *meditate*, especially prominent in Psalm 119.

Both the Old and New Testaments include rich references to a lifestyle of holy noticing. The Old Testament often calls us to remember God's works, while the New Testament calls us to fix our minds on attributes such as love, honor, and truth. Yet the Bible isn't limited to a cognitive understanding of the mind. Functions of the mind also include deciding, judging, feeling, and perceiving. So this way of living isn't just a mental exercise. It's more like a laboratory of the soul to create space for God and His Word.

In Psalm 8:3–4, the psalmist writes,

When I consider your heavens,
    the work of your fingers,
the moon and the stars,
    which you have set in place,
what is mankind that you are mindful of them,
    human beings that you care for them?

This is one of the few places Scripture actually uses the word *mindful*. This question seems to rise off the psalmist's tongue after he ponders creation, which points Him to God's majesty and glory. As he reflects on this, he's amazed that God, the Creator-Sustainer of the universe, has made mankind the unique object of His care, attention, and goodness. And the New Testament describes God's presence and His undying love for us in the life, death, and resurrection of Jesus.

The Greek translation of the Old Testament (the Septuagint) translates the word *mimneske* as "be mindful" or to actively "remember." It's the same word the thief on the cross used when he asked Jesus to remember him. In fact, the word for "mindful" is variously translated as "remember," "be concerned about," "call to mind," and "meditate."[6] This implies personal involvement in the *remembering*, *attention*, and *awareness*, which are all components of holy noticing.

The Hebrew Scriptures often use parallelism, saying the same thing twice with different words. In the verse cited above, David uses both *care* and *mindful*. *Care* includes overtones of hospitality, a trait that a lifestyle of holy noticing can produce in us. And Judaism considered this lifestyle a divine attribute related to God's loving-kindness (*hesed*), which we should emulate.[7]

Two other Hebrew words describe a mindful lifestyle: *haga* and *siach*, most often translated "meditate." They are used to describe silent reflection upon God's works (Ps. 143:5) and upon His Word (Ps. 119:15, 23). By meditating on God's works, the ancient Jew was able to keep God in the forefront of their consciousness.[8]

Creation points to both God's attentiveness and His reflective nature. He brought into being all that is by His creative attention and power. Beauty in creation points to God's mindful attention to detail as well as to His intrinsic beauty. Creation was punctuated by God's pausing to contemplate His work. He rested on the seventh day not because He was tired but to revel in His work and be present with it. He set an example for us to pause, contemplate, and be mindful of Him and His work daily and on a seven-day rhythm of work and rest. And as A. W. Tozer wrote, "God dwells in His creation and is everywhere indivisibly present in all His works."[9]

One of the most often-quoted verses that uses the word *meditate* is Joshua 1:8: "Keep this Book of the Law always on your lips; *meditate* on it day and night, so that you may be careful to do everything written in it. Then you will be prosperous and successful" (emphasis mine). Joshua used this word to describe an essential component in holy noticing: obedience. Holy noticing is not merely an end in itself but includes a double emphasis: stillness before God *and* virtuous action, being fully present in *the moment*, and behaving rightly in the *moments* of life.[10]

King David penned Psalm 62 at a time when others threatened his life. Yet this psalm lacks an overt prayer, one of the few psalms that doesn't contain pleas for deliverance, mercy, or release from danger. Rather, David writes of his deep confidence that God will protect him. He's not ruminating about his future, frightened about the present situation, or anxiously making plans to deal with the danger. He mindfully waits in confident silence. He filled his heart and mind not with tumultuous emotions but with thoughts of God's greatness and promise of refuge.

David models holy noticing in a difficult moment. Just as the early Christians who lived in the Egyptian desert (called the desert fathers and mothers or monastics) repeated what was called the Jesus Prayer to help them become more fully present for God (more on that below), I can envision David repeating, "For God alone my soul waits in silence" as an early form of such a prayer.

> **A mindful life helps us stop and pay attention to both God's Word and His works as we see it in people, in creation, and in our bodies. It counters our busy lives filled with faster internet speeds, speed-reading, and skimming relationships.**

A mindful life helps us stop and pay attention to both God's Word and His works as we see it in people, in creation, and in our bodies. It counters our busy lives filled with faster internet speeds, speed-reading, and skimming relationships. Much like a prism reveals the wide spectrum of the color in light, holy noticing reveals truth to our hearts and "opens us to the mind of God and to his world and presence in the world."[11] It's a spiritual discipline rooted in both God's Word and His works.

In addition to the story about Jesus' visit to Mary and Martha, the New Testament illustrates a mindful lifestyle in other ways. For example, the New Testament word *mneme*, sometimes translated "remember" (Matt. 5:23; Luke 1:72; Luke 23:42) could also be translated as "being mindful" (2 Peter 1:15). Jesus challenged us to "remember" or "be mindful" in Mark 8:17–18:

> Aware of their discussion, Jesus asked them: "Why are you talking about having no bread? Do you still not see or understand? Are your hearts hardened? Do you have eyes but fail to see, and ears but fail to hear? And don't you remember?"

The word for "remember" here is the Greek word *mnemo-neute*, to remember in an enduring way. So we could also read this last question as "And won't you be mindful?"

Jesus also used the phrase, "Whoever has ears, let them hear." He often used these words after He told a parable. He's admonishing His listeners then (and us now) that we must tune out distractions and truly pay attention to Him and His Word, key components in a lifestyle of holy noticing. Even the prophet Isaiah cautions against seeing yet failing to understand and listening but not perceiving (Isa. 6:9–10; 29:10).

Jesus often illustrated His teaching by closely observing nature and the material world. He spoke about salt sprinkled on food, sparrows, little children, yeast mixed with flour, and the growth of tiny seeds. In Matthew 6, He taught against worry by telling His listeners to pay attention to birds and flowers. Jesus lived a holy-noticing lifestyle, noticing things around Him with a holy purpose.

At significant junctures in His life—from the beginning of His public ministry to His transfiguration to His final hours in the garden of Gethsemane—He often withdrew to be still and quiet, focusing on His heavenly Father. He taught about the value of secret prayer in Matthew 6, praying privately when no one was around.

Other New Testament writers also point to holy noticing. James cautions us about the danger of forgetting when he wrote these words:

> Anyone who listens to the word but does not do what it says is like someone who looks at his face in a mirror and, after looking at himself, goes away and immediately forgets what he looks like. But whoever looks intently into the

perfect law that gives freedom, and continues in it—not forgetting what they have heard, but doing it—they will be blessed in what they do. (1:23–25)

He's referring to actively remembering, paying attention—the skills that holy noticing develops in us.

Mind was one of Paul's favorite words. He used it more than forty times in his letters. This reveals that he understood how the mind works in connection to our whole being, long before psychology or neuroscience affirmed these truths. And, he tells us to "pray continually" (1 Thess. 5:17), not so much with a litany of words but as a way of being fully present to God in our minds and circumstances. When he went into the desert after his conversion, Paul became a prototype for the desert monastics who would go into the desert over the following two centuries to develop the contemplative-mindful life.

The early believers gave us other examples of paying attention:

- Simeon and Anna paid attention in the moment, knowing that the Messiah was soon to come (see Luke 2:25–38).

- The shepherds were fully present as they gazed into the face of the baby Jesus (see Luke 2:16).

- The Magi paid attention to the signs God gave them in the sky to travel a great distance to see the Messiah (see Matt. 2:1–2).

- Mary paid attention to the mystery of the super-natural conception of the Son of God (see Luke 1:26–38).

- The Roman centurion paid enough attention to Jesus' crucifixion to exclaim that Jesus was the Son of God (see Mark 15:39).

- And as the early Christians understood that Jesus fulfilled the law, they began to ponder how to meditate on Him. Out of this rose a prayer called the Jesus Prayer that Christians in the first and second century prayed to stay focused on God. It was the earliest recorded example of a way to ponder God. It read simply, "Lord Jesus Christ, Son of God, have mercy on me, a sinner" (see Luke 18:13).

> The ultimate goal in holy noticing is action as we express greater love for Jesus and for others.

The Bible illustrates that the ultimate goal in holy noticing is action as we express greater love for Jesus and for others. Holy noticing helps us live out Jesus' answer to the question posed by a Pharisee about the greatest commandment. Jesus said,

"'Love the Lord your God with all your heart and with all your soul and with all your mind.' This is the first and greatest commandment. And the second is like it: 'Love your neighbor as yourself.'" (Matt. 22:37–39)

Holy Noticing in Church History

Christian history from the past two thousand years provides many examples of believers who developed and practiced this lifestyle of mindfulness or holy noticing. One expert writes,

"Mindfulness was not just a practice of Jesus recovered today but has been a practice of the Church through the centuries, though often neglected and repressed."[12]

Although the term *contemplation* was sometimes the word of choice for this type of Christian spirituality,[13] it was defined as "the action of beholding, or looking at with attention and thought,"[14] significant components in the art of holy noticing.

The Desert Monastics

In the first and second centuries following Jesus' resurrection, the Roman government severely persecuted the church. This prompted many believers to flee into the deserts around Palestine, Syria, and Egypt to seek God. We call these people the desert mothers and fathers, or desert monastics. When Constantine, emperor of Rome, claimed a conversion in AD 312, persecution ended. About seventy years later, Christianity became the official religion of the Roman world and churches rapidly grew.

Unfortunately, the standards of membership were relaxed and many professing Christians began to take on characteristics of the culture. Other believers felt that the cozy relationship between the church and the state resulted in a compromised, diluted, and mediocre faith. So many more left the church and joined the monastics in the desert so they could know God better and keep their faith pure. They organized themselves into communities, established monasteries, and lived ascetic lifestyles while plying their trades and growing their own food. They began to develop a lifestyle of holy noticing reflected in practices such as silence, solitude, and contemplation. By the end of the fourth century, more than thirty thousand monks and nuns lived in the deserts of Lower and Upper Egypt.[15]

They viewed the desert as a place free of distractions and a laboratory to develop their faith, resist temptation, and love Jesus more purely. They learned many psychological insights about the mind, long before psychology existed. They saw precedent in John the Baptist and Jesus, both of whom went into the desert.

Their writings reflect strong themes of holy noticing.[16] Attention—a key skill in this practice—became the foundation of desert spirituality.[17] To them, following Jesus was less about external practices and more about self-knowledge and inner watchfulness. And these early monastics were deeply committed to Scripture. Their lifestyle "took place within the exercise of reading, meditating, preaching, and teaching the biblical text."[18]

They cited biblical examples of Moses's, Elijah's, Elisha's, John the Baptist's, and Jesus' time in the wilderness as inspiration to withdraw into the desert to seek God and fight Satan. Their ultimate goal, as they grew more intimate with God, was to establish a path of discipleship to challenge the compromised faith they believe the established church had embraced.

The disciplines practiced by the desert monastics continued into the Western (Catholic) church, the Eastern (Orthodox) church, and then later into the Protestant church and most recently the evangelical church. And recent discoveries in neuroscience have confirmed the multiple benefits of a mindful lifestyle that the writers of Scripture already knew and the early Christians already practiced.

The early desert monastics and those who followed certainly had their weaknesses. Some created works-based and legalistic steps they believed were necessary for spiritual growth. Some overemphasized emotion at the expense of Scripture.

Some taught obsessively about mystical union with Christ. Some waffled between extreme asceticism, an overemphasis on God's transcendence and unknowability, or an overemphasis on identifying with Jesus' suffering.

However, they all recognized how mental activity could affect their focus on God. Although the mind was God's domain, and demons could not enter the deepest parts of a believer's mind, they still could tempt us. They took their cues from Jesus' response when Satan tempted Him in the wilderness (see Matt. 4:1–11; Luke 4:1). He responded to His temptation with Scripture. To help them avoid the temptation to get caught up with inner dialogue, they developed prayer words or portions of Scripture they would repeat to counter mind wandering.

They practiced several elements of holy noticing, such as cultivating watchfulness, learning to be aware of their thoughts and emotions without commentary, and using their breath as a neutral anchor. I'll explain more about this, as well as the biblical foundation of the breath in the next chapter.[19]

They based their practice on four key Bible passages, which also provide a basis for practicing holy noticing today.[20]

- **1 Thessalonians 5:17**—"Pray continually." They saw this as a spirit of prayer carried around in their hearts, a watchful disposition as a constant mindfulness of God's presence.

- **Romans 8:6**—"The mind governed by the flesh is death, but the mind governed by the Spirit is life and peace." This was their ultimate aim.

- **Romans 12:2**—"Do not conform to the pattern of this world, but be transformed by the renewing of your mind. Then you will be able to test and approve what God's will is—his good, pleasing and perfect will." This reflected a mind unconditioned by the world, like that of a child's mind, simple and nonjudgmental.

- **2 Corinthians 10:5**—"We take captive every thought to make it obedient to Christ." This illustrated the spiritual work to free their minds from conditioned patterns of thinking. This process, called *anachoresis*, was a concept that described how they could bring the mind back from thoughts about the past or the future to the mind of Christ.

Later Historical Influencers Who Illustrate a Mindful Lifestyle

Although hundreds of committed Christians from early Christian history practiced and wrote on a lifestyle of holy noticing, a few stand out. You can download a more comprehensive timeline at www.holynoticing.com/bonus.

Origen of Alexandria (AD 185–254) was the third-century early church scholar who wrote that the most important factor in understanding the spiritual life was attention,[21] a key aspect of holy noticing. Scattered throughout the writings of St. Augustine of Hippo (AD 354–430) are insights that emphasize our need to be aware of our thoughts.

John Calvin (1509–1564), one of the most influential theologians in Christian history, began his famous theological treatise, *Institutes,* by writing about self-awareness (knowledge of self), an essential component of holy noticing.[22] For Calvin, faith included both theological correctness and a strong emotional heart connection.[23] Martin Luther (1483–1546) began the Protestant Reformation and was greatly influenced by several of the earlier writers who wrote about what we're calling holy noticing.[24] He even said that one book (*German Theology*) influenced him so much that with the exception of the Bible and Augustine's work, he learned more from that book than any other.[25] He recommended three rules for Scripture reading: (1) *oratio* (start with prayer), (2) *meditatio* (meditate, think deeply and carefully muse), and (3) *tentatio* (deal with the spiritual attacks of dread, despair, and anxiety that believers face),[26] all aspects reflected in holy noticing.

John Wesley (1703–1791) founded Methodism and promoted what he called "watchfulness," a spiritual posture to help believers be alert to God in all things. He practiced and taught a way of life to prayerfully attend to the working of God in every moment. D. L. Moody (1837–1899) owned and cited several books written by ancient and modern Christian contemplatives (those who practiced holy noticing) such as Madame Guyon and Thomas à Kempis.[27] And pastor and devotional writer A. W. Tozer (1897–1963) quotes and alludes to thirty-five contemplative writers in a positive way.[28]

We've seen how both Scripture and Christian history provide a strong foundation and source for a lifestyle of holy noticing. So what comes next? How can mindfulness practice help me grow closer to Christ, deepen my relationships, and give me greater peace when my emotions go awry? That's what you'll discover in the next few chapters as I unpack the BREATHe model.

Bonus material available at www.holynoticing.com/bonus:

• Mindfulness Church History Timeline.

CHAPTER 3

The BREATHe Model: The Six Bible-Based Practices of Holy Noticing

Let the remembrance of Jesus be with your every breath.
Then indeed you will appreciate the value of stillness.
—ST. JOHN CLIMACUS

Our meditation must be directed toward God;
otherwise we may spend our time of retiral in quiet
converse with ourselves. This may quiet our nerves
but will not further our spiritual life in any way.
—A. W. TOZER

Before our first child was born, my wife and I enrolled in childbirth classes at the local hospital. We all sat on dainty pillows spread on the floor as the lecturer held up plastic models of babies in the womb, showed us nauseating pictures of births, and explained in gory detail what happens when babies are born. Ever since I was the new kid in town and almost passed out in my sixth-grade class while we watched a movie that showed a beating cow's heart, I have avoided blood at all costs. So during the childbirth classes, I was most interested to know what happened if husbands pass out during delivery. I was pretty sure I would.

I don't remember what the instructor said, but I made a decision that precluded any chance that I might pass out.

When our first was born, I sat in the waiting room and read two-year-old copies of *Field & Stream* magazine. However, I do clearly remember one concept from that class—breathing techniques while the mom is in labor. Supposedly, husbands could help their wives endure contractions better by deep breathing, in-out, in-out, in-out.

Well, during labor at the hospital, the breathing techniques didn't go as planned. I almost passed out from hyperventilating as I tried to help Sherryl breathe—in-out, in-out, in-out. And my wife was not exactly her normal sweet self. I didn't fan her face fast enough to keep her cool. So she punched me in the stomach. She has a wicked punch.

She finally asked for an epidural.

Things got much better.

I must have done something wrong with the breathing technique. Maybe I created some extra stress when I asked her if I could turn on the TV in the hospital room and watch Monday Night Football. I thought that would distract her from the pain and work better than breathing in-out, in-out, in-out.

She thought different.

I missed Monday Night Football that night.

Even though the breathing technique didn't work for us in childbirth, incorporating breath into a lifestyle of holy noticing does work (I could have used it that night). Using your breath as you learn this lifestyle has biblical, historical, scientific, and pragmatic roots I will explain below.

The Bible and Your Breath

The Bible often mentions breath. The book of Genesis tells us that, at creation, God "breathed into his [Adam's] nostrils the breath of life, and the man became a living being" (Gen. 2:7). The Hebrew word there for "breath" is *ruach* and can mean "breath," "wind," or "spirit." God animated mankind with His breath. The Scriptures use breath as a unique sign and symbol of mankind, using it to distinguish human creation from the rest of creation.

Job mentions that the breath of God gave him life, spiritual vitality, and understanding: "The Spirit of God has made me; the breath of the Almighty gives me life" (Job 33:4). The psalmist reflects this idea in Psalm 104:29–30:

> When you hide your face,
>   they are terrified;
> when you take away their breath,
>   they die and return to the dust.
> When you send your Spirit,
>   they are created,
>   and you renew the face of the ground.

When Elijah once hid in a cave after an intensive spiritual battle, he heard the "faint sound of breathing," both His own breath and the breath or whisper of God. In a prophecy meant to give hope to Israel, he also describes God animating a valley of dry bones with His breath (Ezek. 37).

One ancient Jewish prayer practice was to inhale and exhale on every letter of the Hebrew word for God's covenant name, YHWH. This word for the name of God was actually breathed because the Jews viewed God's name as unspeakable.

The New Testament also uses the word *pneuma* (breath), which correlates to the Hebrew word *ruach*. When Jesus first appeared to the early disciples after He rose from the dead, He gave them the Holy Spirit when He breathed on them. "And with that he breathed on them and said, 'Receive the Holy Spirit'" (John 20:22). Just as God brought physical life to Adam with His breath, so does the breath or Spirit of Jesus give us spiritual life.

Our English word *spiritual* comes from the Latin word *spiritualis*, which means "of breathing." And fundamentally, holy noticing is a *spiritual* practice, which disposes us to allow something to take place.[1] Sailors can't produce wind to push their boat. They simply use their skills to harness the wind's power. Likewise, developing skills in holy noticing help us harness the "breath" of the Spirit, His power, to deepen our relationship with Jesus.

I based my BREATHe model on a verse about Jesus, along with some neuroscience support. The verse Luke 2:52 reads, "Jesus grew in wisdom and stature, and in favor with God and man." This verse about His life suggested four broad categories:

- *Wisdom* relates to our thinking and emotions.

- *Stature* correlates to our physical bodies.

- *In favor with God* relates to our spiritual selves,
  our souls.

- *In favor with man* points to our relationships.

Neuroscientists have discovered similar areas that a lifestyle of mindfulness affects: "your body state (your activity level), your cognitive state (your thoughts), your emotional state (your feelings), and your relationship state (how you relate to yourself and others)."[2] And a lifestyle of holy noticing can actually alter our brain's pathways in these areas in a positive way.[3]

So, I developed my BREATHe model to include these components: the physical (our bodies, the *B*), people (our relationships, the *R*), emotions (affect, afflictive emotions, the *A*), our mental lives (thinking, the *T*), and our spirits (heart, the *H*). I added one additional component, *E* for environment, because holy noticing includes paying attention to God's handiwork around us—the sights, sounds, and objects in our environment. And of course, the final letter, *e* (engage the world like Christ), is the most important because it represents living a holy-noticing lifestyle.

As a kid, I often watched *Tarzan* on TV on Saturday mornings (that sounds very old, because it is). An actor named Johnny Weissmuller played Tarzan in this ancient black-and-white TV show. The jungle animals were his friends. When the monkeys sensed danger, they'd howl and swing from tree to tree, making the trees seem to come alive. *Monkey mind* is a term often used to describe how our mind easily flits from one thought to the next. Our minds seem to constantly chatter at us with thoughts often unrelated to the task at hand (like when our mind wanders during prayer). And the more we pay attention to that chatter, the more distracting it becomes.

The ancient Christians who practiced holy noticing understood how this chattering mind distracted spiritual focus. So they gave the mind something to do—focus on a short word or a biblical phrase while coupling it to awareness of the breath itself. It's something akin to a mental piece of red string tied around your finger to jog your mind when it drifts.[4]

They prescribed various Scripture verses as antidotes to different kinds of distracting thoughts. They viewed these afflictive thoughts as opportunities to immerse themselves in Scripture and prayer. As a result, the kinds of prayers and

Scriptures helped quiet those thoughts.[5] One ancient Christian wrote, "Let the name of Jesus adhere to your breath, and then you will know the blessings of stillness."[6] He noticed that if you incorporated the breath into a holy-noticing practice, you could quiet distracting thoughts.

The Jesus Prayer became common. It combined two Scriptures—"Son of David, have mercy on me!" (Luke 18:39) and "God, have mercy on me, a sinner" (Luke 18:13). As you breathe in, you would pray, *Jesus, Son of David*. As you breathed out, you would pray, *Have mercy on me, a sinner*. This prayer acknowledged that part of the one praying wanted to be in God's presence and part of him didn't. So, the Jesus Prayer became a plea for help and a practical way to keep their attention on the Lord or to bring their attention back to Him. Pairing the Jesus Prayer or a prayer word with our breath is a helpful tool to bring our attention back from mind wandering to the present moment with the Lord.[7]

One way to see the value of this is to imagine you're sitting at a café with a friend. As you chat, the honks of a car divert your attention for a moment. You want to be courteous to your friend by giving her your attention. You might say something like, "As I was saying," to focus your attention back on the conversation. You're not trying to stop the road noise. Rather, you want to return to the conversation. In a like manner, a prayer word tied to the breath helps us place our attention back to our practice when our mind wanders.[8]

Short two-to-three-word prayers tied to my breath have often helped quiet my roving mind in my daily devotional practices and have helped when I take short mental breaks throughout the day. It's a simple way to apply Paul's instruction in 2 Corinthians 10:5: "Take captive every thought to make it obedient to Christ."

The prayer phrase I've picked is *Holy Spirit, breathe on me*. It's simply an easy-to-remember prayer I've chosen that reminds me that the Holy Spirit already dwells in me. You'll eventually pick your own

> As we use these prayer words to bring us back to our breath and focus on the Lord, we must not let them become mechanical repetitions against which Jesus cautions (see Matt. 6:7).

simple prayer. On the in-breath, I say, *Holy Spirit,* and with the outbreath, *breathe on me.* This short prayer serves as a biblical anchor to bring my mind to attention and to avoid getting caught up in distracting thoughts. Yet, as we use these prayer words to bring us back to our breath and focus on the Lord, we must not let them become mechanical repetitions against which Jesus cautions (see Matt. 6:7). Remind yourself that the purpose behind your repetition is to bring your wandering mind back to thoughts of Jesus. Sometimes I expand on these prayers by praying the name *Lord Jesus* or *Heavenly Father* on the in-breath and praying some quality of the Trinity on the out-breath, such as *my Redeemer* or *my Rock.* This type of praying can become a very enriching way to pray.

The Science behind Our Breath

If we live into our seventies, we will have taken almost a billion breaths, and the weight of the air we breathe would weigh almost three hundred tons.[9] And our breathing affects our nervous system and our emotions, as neuroscientist Dr. Alex Korb explains:

Breathing affects the brain through signals carried by the vagus nerve. Not only does the vagus nerve send signals down to the heart . . . but it also carries signals up into the brain stem. Vagus nerve signaling is important in activating circuits for resting and relaxation, known as the parasympathetic nervous system. The parasympathetic system is the opposite of the sympathetic nervous system, which controls the fight-or-flight instinct. Slow breathing increases activity in the vagus nerve and pushes the brain toward parasympathetic activity. So slow, deep breathing calms you down.[10]

Eighty percent of the fibers in this nerve runs from our internal organs (our belly, heart, lungs, and intestines) to the back of our brain. So, breathing is a way we can train our arousal system[11] and minimize problems that come from unchecked anger, depression, and anxiety.[12] Slow, focused breathing literally calms our minds and bodies. That was the science behind our childbirth classes. We simply didn't grasp the idea at the time.

Our breath is something that is always with us and, for most of us, is neutral. It's also a good barometer of our current mental and emotional state. And since our minds struggle to be still, focusing on something neutral such as breath gives our wandering minds something to do.

Remember that one goal of holy noticing is to help us live in the present moment with the Lord and with others. Since our thoughts are naturally scattered (like the agitated monkeys in Tarzan's jungle), we need something that can provide an anchor for our attention. Refocusing on our breath gives us that neutral anchor upon which to place our attention, which in turn strengthens our ability to focus our attention.[13] Studies also show that when we're emotionally distressed, returning to a neutral anchor such as the breath calms us down.[14] In the past, scientists measured mindfulness with self-report inventories. However, they now use a more accurate method in the lab to measure it—how many breaths a person can count before their mind starts to wander.[15] Try it sometime and you'll discover how hard it is before your mind wanders.

Our Breath and Practical Considerations

Our breath comes into unique play when we focus on something that requires concentrated effort. When we thread a needle or try to move a tray of glasses filled with liquid, our breath tends to slow and deepen without our realizing it. Swimmers, runners, and concert pianists understand the importance of the final deep breath the moment before the gun starts a race or before they begin a concerto. And, ultimately, our breath reminds us that God has given us life.

When our mind wanders, the common word *BREATHe* makes it easier to remember to return to both our breath and to the particular skill of the BREATHe model we were practicing, without using a lot of mental resources. When your mind wanders as you practice holy noticing (and it will), it takes mental effort to return to what you were thinking about. In fact, our mind wanders almost half of our waking hours.[16] Our mind wanders because our brain cells tire after spending only twelve seconds on a task that requires our attention. Those cells then begin to look for new energy. If they can't immediately access more energy, mind wandering begins.[17] However, given time and practice, you can counter your mind's tendency to wander.

The BREATHe acronym helps us more easily return to the previous spot when our minds stray. We already use acronyms as memory shortcuts for many words and concepts such as APB (all points bulletin), MIA (missing in action), BFF (best friend forever), LOL (laugh out loud), and even one for prayer—ACTS (adoration, confession, thanksgiving, and supplication).

Here's how the acronym BREATHe can help you. Let's say during your daily devotions when you are practicing holy noticing that you are at the *E* (environment) and you're listening deeply to the sounds around you. Without being aware of it, your mind wanders to the pile of clothes on the floor in your bedroom that need dry cleaning. That thought jumps to, *Maybe I can drop them off at the dry cleaners on the way to work.* And that thought reminds you about the project due to your boss at ten that morning. By now your mind is off to the races. You may have mind wandered for a few seconds or a few minutes before you finally realize how far off track your thoughts have strayed. The BREATHe acronym helps you easily get back to the point where your mind began to wander.

Your internal dialogue might go something like this: *Oh, boy. My mind has wandered off* again.

Simply go back to your breath as an anchor and take a couple of deep slow breaths while you repeat your anchor prayer. Then you'd silently ask yourself, *Now where was I?* B . . . R . . . E . . . *oh yeah. That's where I was, on* E, *the environment.*

You're now back on track without having expended too much mental energy to recall where you were. When you realized your mind wandered, you first went back to your breath as your neutral anchor and then to your breath prayer. Then, you used the acronym BREATHe to get you back to the spot in your holy-noticing practice when your mind wandered off.

Your mind will flit from one thought to another, even during your daily practice. Sometimes I will thank God for reminding me that my mind wandered. When your mind wanders, and it often will, don't berate yourself, because you'll needlessly use up mental energy. When it strays, simply bring it back to the breath and your prayer. Given time, this practice will help you realize more quickly when your mind has wandered and actually reduce how often your mind will wander. And there is nothing special about the order of the components in BREATHe. But when you follow the order of the acronym, you'll more easily get back to where you were when your mind got off track.

As I explained earlier, each letter of the BREATHe model represents a core practice in holy noticing. And although the benefits of each practice overlap, each one tends to offer a unique benefit, which I unpack in later chapters. Within each practice I suggest a skill or two. The BREATHe model also incorporates the power of Scripture as we fill our minds with thoughts of Him through His Word.

Scripture is the foundation for holy noticing. For each of the six practices in the BREATHe model, I have suggested anchor verses related to that particular practice. You may want to pick different ones. Whichever verses you choose, it's best to memorize them so they're easy to retrieve from memory without much mental effort. But you don't have to wait until you've memorized them to begin to practice.

Joshua 1:8 tells us to meditate on God's Word. The word *meditate* was used to describe cows who "chewed the cud" to break down their food to maximize its nutrients. When we ruminate over Scripture, the Holy Spirit helps us break it down so that it sinks deep into our soul.

As you begin to learn the six practices, slowly and reflectively bring to mind each anchor Scripture. Your purpose is not to mindlessly read or quote Scripture. Rather, it's to contemplate and immerse yourself in God's truth as you do the skill associated with that particular practice.

Before I unpack each one, consider these suggestions as you begin your practice of holy noticing.

First, find a place in your home that is quiet, undisturbed, and free from distractions. I do my daily devotional practices in a room with a window that overlooks some trees in our backyard. It's private and quiet. Any place in your home or apartment would work, even a cleared-out area in a large closet.

Second, posture does matter. I suggest sitting in a chair that is comfortable but not too comfortable. A fully extended La-Z-Boy recliner won't be as conducive for your experience as it would be for sleep. So choose a chair that supports your back well. Sit up straight. Sometimes I fold my hands together in my lap. Sometimes I place them palms up to remind me of my submission before the Lord.

Third, decide whether to practice with your eyes open or closed. Either option will work. Closing your eyes minimizes distractions because we tend to think about what we see. However, when I am at the _E_ (environment) portion of the BREATHe practice, I will often open my eyes. Because I sit in front of a window where I can see trees, I am able to revel in God's creation as I observe the changing seasons, watch a sunrise, or observe a pair of birds.

Fourth, determine how long you will practice holy noticing in your devotional time. And remember, it's not *just* a devotional practice. It should be a lifestyle. I suggest starting with three minutes a day the first week, and then as you learn each practice, add three minutes more each week. So then within six weeks, when you combine all the practices, you'll work up to about twenty minutes a day. In my morning practice, which I follow five days a week, I set my phone to alert me after twenty minutes and then I stop when the alarm goes off.

Fifth, use your Bible to read your anchor verses. Even better, memorize them so you don't have to look them up each time.

Sixth, prepare your heart. Holy noticing is not a technique to "turn on" the presence of God[18] but a way we can tell God we are there to be with Him. It's not a matter of striving or forcing but being present. When you pull the stopper from a tub, you don't have to force the water down the drain. It simply flows out. Likewise, holy noticing is an act of intention, a posture indicating you are attending to God's presence. It should not be forced.

Seventh, try to eliminate as many distractions as you can and begin with slow, deep breath prayers. Tricia McCary Rhodes writes,

> You may want to envision breathing in God's presence, love, kindness, hope, peace, and so on, then breathing out your restlessness, distraction, mind-wandering, and the like. Let your breaths be measured; focus on how your body feels as you slow it down. . . .
>
> As emotions, sensations, or thoughts come up during this time, gently let them move through your heart and mind, and offer them to the Lord for safekeeping. Don't try

to analyze or edit or even judge these, but simply let God take them, knowing that he will give you what you need during this time.[19]

Of course, if the Holy Spirit convicts you of some sin, first confess it and then return to quiet presence before Him.

Finally, start slowly and build one practice upon the next. Practice the first component for a week, and then add the second component to it the second week, the third component the third week, and so on. In the final chapter, I suggest a six-week plan to help you build the full BREATHe model into your spiritual routine and appendix A guides you through a full BREATHe session. Don't let discouragement hinder you. With practice, these skills will become easier and you'll greatly benefit from them.

So, how do you practice holy noticing?

In the following chapters, I'll answer that question as I unpack each part of the BREATHe model, keeping in mind our definition of holy noticing: *noticing, with a holy purpose, God and His handiwork, our relationships, and our inner world of thoughts and feelings.*

PART 2

"LOOKING UP AND OUT": GOD, HIS HANDIWORK, AND OUR RELATIONSHIPS

CHAPTER 4

Practice One: Ponder and Yield Your Body

*I praise you because I am fearfully and wonderfully made;
your works are wonderful, I know that full well.*
—PSALM 139:14

Reality is the leading cause of stress for those in touch with it.
—LILY TOMLIN

CHAPTER BIG IDEA: This chapter explains the first practice in the BREATHe mindfulness model, *B*, which stands for "Ponder and Yield Your *Body*." You'll learn how to use two skills to reduce the harmful effects on your body from chronic stress, which can hinder our relationship with God.

SO WHAT DOES HOLY NOTICING HAVE to do with stress and our bodies?

It's simple.

Our bodies matter to God.

And chronic stress harms our bodies.

Chronic stress, the kind that keeps us on high alert for long periods of time, can be deadly. It's an epidemic today with seven in ten Americans suffering from some physical problem related to it.[1] And approximately 60 percent of doctor visits are due to stress-related issues.[2] Chronic stress even shrinks parts of our brains,[3] especially areas involved in memory, and it grows the part of our brains behind fear and anxiety.[4]

Choices we make can magnify the harm that stress causes. Our mental and physical response to such stress can hinder spiritual growth. Yet holy noticing reduces the negative effects stress places on our bodies, which in turn can foster spiritual growth.

The Scriptures reflect the high value God places on our bodies, with perhaps the clearest arguments coming from the pen of Paul. One of his favorite images was the human body. He called the church "the body of Christ" (Rom. 7:4). He describes spiritual gifts by using a body as a metaphor (1 Cor. 12). He tells us to "offer your bodies as a living sacrifice" (Rom. 12:1). He even describes our bodies as temples of the Holy Spirit: "Do you not know that your bodies are temples of the Holy Spirit?" (1 Cor. 6:19). In the next verse, he commands us to "honor God with your bodies." These words *honor, temple,* and *sacrifice* reinforce our responsibility to make wise choices that will keep our bodies healthy, to the best of our ability. These choices certainly include healthy eating, regular exercise, and adequate sleep. But for the purposes of this first holy-noticing practice, "*B*: Ponder and Yield Your *Body*," these choices encompass how we respond to stress in our minds and hearts as they relate to our bodies.

God gave each of us a human body for life on earth. The body is suited to live on earth as we "honor God" (1 Cor. 6:20) with it and treat it as a "living sacrifice" (Rom. 12:1). God as Creator even calls the human body and all creation "very good" (Gen. 1:31). And King David even marveled at how magnificently God created the human body (see Ps. 139:14).

Since our bodies matter to God, they should matter to us as well. As we ponder and yield our bodies through the lifestyle of holy noticing, we demonstrate appropriate care for them and lessen the effects from chronic stress. When our bodies work better because we respond in healthy ways to stress, we can serve God more effectively and love others more consistently.

In this chapter, we'll examine how this first holy-noticing practice in the BREATHe model can combat the effects from stress. The place to start is to understand how the body responds to stress.

Your Body and the Stress Response

A prune-sized part of your brain, the insula, makes you aware of your internal body states and feelings such as trust, empathy, guilt, and disgust.[5] It's involved in giving you your "gut feelings."[6] I believe the Holy Spirit often engages this part of our brains through intuition about ourselves and others. The apostle Paul picked up on this internal sensitivity when he wrote, "Dear friends, do not believe every spirit, but test the spirits to see whether they are from God, because many false prophets have gone out into the world" (1 John 4:1).

Your brain's alarm system includes the almond-shaped amygdala, the brain's "feeler," that kick-starts the stress response and tags memories connected to emotion. Think of an imaginary pink Post-it note attached to an emotional memory in your brain of a time in first grade when you were deeply embarrassed. Your feeler allows you to recall and relive negative emotional moments and actually feel those same emotions even decades later. You recall negative emotional experiences more often and more quickly than positive emotional experiences because negative emotions have bigger and brighter neural Post-it notes attached. Some have described this process by saying that *bad (emotion) is stronger than good (emotion).*[7]

More neural pathways travel from your amygdala to the front part of your brain (your brain's CEO/conductor/general[8]) than vice versa. And its central location gives it the proximity to quickly influence your body's stress response (and your reactivity), operating five times faster than your CEO.[9] This gives it an unfair advantage in a *reason* versus *emotion* tug-of-war. Emotion wins too often. It's also quick at feeling, yet poor at making accurate judgments. Your brain's feeler sometimes incites anxiety through unconscious associations in your memory, rather than relying on logic. This process is behind post-traumatic stress disorder or PTSD. That's why we can get anxious or fearful for no apparent reason.

The smell of popcorn balls can make me feel nauseated. It wasn't until later in life that I remembered why. As a ten-year-old kid, I once got violently sick after eating a popcorn ball. My feeler had stored that emotional memory, but my CEO had not yet made the connection.

As sinister as the feeler may sound, we need it. Although it can sometimes hijack clear thinking and godly behavior, God gave us this as a survival tool to help us appropriately respond to danger. If a car pulls in front of you at an intersection, you don't want to waste time consciously thinking about slamming on the brakes before you actually do. You want your brain to instantly tell your foot to press the brake pedal, NOW! Another benefit of your feeler is that it also emotionally stamps pleasant emotions, although those memories only get the smaller neural Post-its.

Another part of your brain that indirectly impacts emotion and your body is your brain's 'rememberer,' a seahorse-shaped collection of brain cells called the hippocampus. This part of the brain stores short-term memories and turns them into long-term ones.[10]

So how do all these parts affect the stress response in your body?

Your body's wiring, the nervous system, includes two sub-systems involved in stress: your brain's emotional *accelerator*[11] and your brain's emotional *brake*.[12] Your accelerator causes emotional fires, and your brake puts them out. They work in tandem, like a seesaw. And when your accelerator revs up too much and for too long (chronic stress), problems ensue.

In a stressful situation when your brain thinks you're in danger, whether real (while on a camping trip, you hear a hungry bear snacking on the bag of Cheetos you left outside your tent) or imagined (your Cheetos-loving boss just ordered you into his office), here's what happens: your feeler quickly signals your emotional accelerator to snap to. Because your emotions are stronger, they can force your CEO off-line and diminish your ability to think clearly. And during stress, the accelerator automatically creates these physiological changes in your body without your intentional effort:

- Adrenaline gets released into your bloodstream to give you more energy, in case you need to fight or flee a bear, whether real or imagined.

- Your brain instantly releases chemicals that increase your attention and shunt blood from less essential areas, such as your skin, to more crucial ones like your muscles (to help you run from that bear).

- Your heart beats faster and blood pressure rises to send more blood to your muscles for the same reason, to fight or flee danger.

- Breathing increases so that more oxygen flows into your brain to maximize alertness and attention.

- You can hear better, and your eyes dilate so you can see better.

- You may sweat, get goose bumps or dry mouth, or feel as if you need to go the bathroom, right then.

- Your feeler becomes more activated, which makes you defensive or reactive.

Again, this happens whether you are truly in danger or you are simply imagining it. Your fight-flight system works on your behalf in real danger. It works against you in imaginary danger.

The second step of the stress response occurs when that stressor doesn't quickly go away. Another brain system kicks in that we can visualize as three dominoes close to one another standing on end. When one domino falls, it makes another one fall, which in turn makes another one fall.[13] If a danger continues, chemicals cascade down from one of these brain parts to the next and finally to the one that releases cortisol, the stress hormone, into your bloodstream. It helps the body maintain steady supplies of blood sugar for fuel and quick energy, and keeps your body in the fight-flight mode. However, when the threat passes, the brain's brake dampens the stress response initiated by the accelerator. It puts the fire out and you experience calm.[14]

In short, that's what happens when your body is stressed.

And the practices you will learn in holy noticing will help minimize the negative effects from chronic stress.

How Holy Noticing Benefits Our Bodies

Research is uncovering multiple benefits that this lifestyle brings to our physical health. One benefit is that it helps us become more aware of what's happening *in* our bodies. That awareness can work like an early warning system to clue us to stress-caused unhealthy thoughts and emotions that, if left unchecked, could harm us over the long term.

Chronic stress damages our bodies through the long-term effects from the stress hormone, cortisol. Practicing holy noticing can, in some cases, decrease the amount of cortisol in our bloodstream.[15] It also increases brain density (gray matter) in areas involved in memory, learning, problem solving, conflict monitoring,[16] emotional self-awareness, and self-regulation.[17] It can even help improve our sleep.[18]

One of the most exciting new neuroscience findings involves its effects on inflammation, now considered a key marker in many chronic diseases. In one study, participants who went through a three-day mindfulness retreat (and practiced several holy-noticing skills, though in a secular setting) showed a decrease in a biomarker of inflammation compared to a control group.[19] Another study showed a direct link between this practice and reduced genetic markers associated with inflammation.[20] Again, science simply informs us what may happen as we practice holy noticing. It does not transform us. God does.

Another exciting finding involves a key measure of health

called heart rate variability (HRV). HRV measures the varia-
tion between each heartbeat. A higher HRV is generally considered a measure of good health. For those who struggle with
anxiety, holy noticing is associated with a higher HRV.[21]

Finally, a mindful lifestyle may actually help us live longer
by slowing the aging process.[22] At the end of our chromosomes
lie protective caps, like plastic caps at the end of shoelaces.
They're called telomeres and are linked to longevity. The longer
and healthier your telomeres, all else being equal, the longer
you tend to live. Chronic stress apparently shortens them.
Telomerase is an enzyme (a catalyst that brings about a chemical reaction) that slows the shortening of these telomeres. Some
studies show that those who practice this mindful lifestyle have
more telomerase, a good indicator of a longer life span.

An Overview of the Holy-Noticing Process

Although each practice in the BREATHe model will initially
require your attention and effort, over time, they will become
second nature. And there is no one right way to practice it.
Keep it simple and remember the definition of holy noticing:
*the art of noticing, with a holy purpose, God and His handi-
work, our relationships, and our inner world of thoughts and
feelings.*

When you begin your daily practice, start by sitting in a
comfortable chair (but not too comfortable), in a place free
from distraction, and focus on your breath, your neutral anchor. Listen to the rhythm of your breath, both the in-breath
and the out-breath. As you breathe, pray a breath prayer
such as *Holy Spirit* (on the in-breath), *breathe on me* (on the
out-breath).

Next, transition your thoughts from the breath prayer to the first practice in the BREATHe model—"*B*: Ponder and Yield Your *Body*." Take note of your body's sensations. Do you feel tired? Are you sore or achy? Does your back hurt? Are you feeling restless? Reflect on your anchor verses. I've recommended several verses for each practice, but you can also choose your own. I have found it helpful to memorize my anchor verses so I can close my eyes and block visual distractions, thus reducing the mental resources I need. I'm then able to be more present with the Lord.

Next, move into the particular skill(s) associated with the practice. I will give you a word picture and a related graphic for each practice to help you easily recall the related skill. After you learn about all the practices and put them together, you'll easily transition from one to the next until you move through all six practices. If you don't make it through all six on a particular day, that's okay. Remember, there's no one right way to practice holy noticing.

As I explained in the previous chapter, I recommend working up to around three minutes per practice. This will mean fifteen to twenty minutes of daily practice when you put them all together, an amount neuroscientists say can bring the most tangible benefits.[23] The key, however, is consistency rather than length.

Ultimately, the goal is to make holy noticing a trait of your day-to-day life. By incorporating these practices into your daily devotional time, you will become adept in living a mindful lifestyle. Try each practice in small bites, three to five minutes at a time for several days until you get more comfortable with each. You may want to return to the corresponding chapter in the book and reread it for a refresher. At first your practice may feel a bit rote. But after a few practice sessions, it will become more natural and automatic, like learning to drive a car.

Below is an example of what a holy-noticing session might look like, including the thoughts, prayers, and activities you might choose for that particular practice. You can download this chart at www.holynoticing.com/bonus to keep in front of you as you learn.

Holy Noticing: Practice Outline

1. Focus on your breath . . .
2. Pray your breath prayer . . .
3. Start with the first letter in the BREATHe model, *B* for "Body" . . .
4. Reflect on your anchor verse(s) related to that practice . . .
5. Do the related skill (recall the related word picture if it helps) . . .
6. Move to the next letter and repeat.

- *B*: **Ponder and Yield Your** *Body*
(skills: body scan, gratefulness exercises)
- *R*: Review and Renew Your *Relationships*
(skills: concentric circles exercise)
- *E*: Notice and Engage Your *Environment*
(skills: deep listening, focused observation exercises)
- *A*: Label and Release Your *Afflictive* Emotions (*Affect*)
(skills: emotional crosshairs, quiet waters exercises)
- *T*: Observe and Submit Your *Thoughts*
(skills: thinking about your thinking exercise)
- *H*: Search and Surrender Your *Heart*
(skills: openheartedness, spiritual vulnerability exercise)

Formal Practice > *B*: Ponder and Yield Your *Body*
Anchor verses: Psalm 139:14; 1 Corinthians 6:19–20; Romans 12:1

Skills: body scan, gratefulness exercises

The first key skill in this practice is called a body scan. Several years ago, my doctor was concerned that I wasn't getting enough calcium to keep my bones strong, so he ordered a bone scan. When I went in for the scan, a radiologist first injected a small amount of radioactive material into my vein. Then as I lay still on a special bed, an X-ray scanner slowly moved over my entire body, from the bottom of my feet to the top of my head, and took a picture of my entire skeletal structure. Fortunately, my bones were fine.

The body scan we use in holy noticing is similar. It's a method we can use to enhance interoception, which is the ability God gave us to feel or sense our inner body states such as hunger, thirst, emotions, intuition (gut feelings), and even our spiritual and relational yearnings. The body scan helps hone this ability to notice our inner body states.[24]

To begin, imagine a camera or scanner moving slowly over your body and taking images, beginning with your left leg, moving to your right leg, then your torso, then your left arm, right arm, and finally moving through your neck and out your head. As you do the body scan, pausing at various places along the way to become more aware of sensations in your body, you will experience two benefits.

First, a body scan can help you become more attuned to where in your body you might be holding stress or tension. My stress tends to show up in my shoulders. A body scan can make me aware that I am hunching my shoulders, which makes my muscles tense. I then can take specific actions to release that tension, such as relaxing or stretching my shoulders. This simple body awareness and body adjustment helps decrease the negative effects of stress on my body. I do this before I speak each Sunday, which helps me communicate more effectively.

A second and related skill is the gratefulness exercise. As you do your body scan, pause and reflect on God's amazing creativity and handiwork by thanking Him for your body. Express gratitude and praise as David did when he wrote, "I praise you because I am fearfully and wonderfully made; your works are wonderful, I know that full well" (Ps. 139:14). In my practice, I have thanked God specifically for such things as the flexibility in my ankle, toenails that protect my toes, and the amazing way all my body organs work seamlessly together to keep me healthy. The gratefulness exercise offers an almost unlimited opportunity to show God gratitude.

Gratefulness benefits us in many ways, including increased positive mood; lower risk of depression; decreased likelihood of anxiety disorders, making us less materialistic;[25] and lasting benefits to our brains.[26] Practicing gratefulness in our thought lives can even change our happiness set point, a baseline of happiness that psychologists once said was unchangeable.[27] As one famous philosopher pointed out, "think" and "thank" share a common heritage. He taught that a "thinking that is thanking" was the best way to think.[28]

The apostle Paul reminded us in Philippians 4:8 to set our minds on that which is good. And he used the words *thanks* and *thanksgiving* more than fifty times in his writings. He usually used the word that combines two Greek words, *eu* ("good") plus *charis* ("grace"). He viewed gratefulness as a thread of God's gracious hand in everything, not as a technique to make us feel better, even though gratefulness does feel good.

Before you begin your first practice, you'll want to read through the sample practice below and the suggested anchor verses. For each practice session, I'll use this same written template style. I write in *italics* what you may *think, verbalize,* or *pray* during the practice session, and I put in [brackets] my comments and suggestions. In this example, I will insert my breath prayers as well as other personal components as if I were doing the practice myself.

Now you are ready. Get comfortable, start your timer for three to five minutes, and close your eyes to visually block out distractions.

As you become more comfortable with this practice, you'll learn to pause long enough to notice physical sensations in your body.

Ponder and Yield Your *Body*—Practice

[Begin with long, slow breaths.
Breathe in.
Breathe out.
Breathe in.
Breathe out.
Breathe in and breathe out with your breath prayer.]

Holy Spirit [the in-breath]
Breathe on me [the out-breath]

[Repeat your breath prayer as long as you want. You may want to include other breath prayers such as *Lord Jesus* (on the in-breath) *You are good* (on the out-breath).]
[Move on to your anchor verses.]

Lord, I come before You and present my body to You. I want to ponder it and yield it to You right now.

[Meditate on your anchor verses, or read them if you have not memorized them.]

Lord, I acknowledge that I am fearfully and wonderfully made. I know that full well.
I acknowledge that my body is a temple of the Holy Spirit that You have freely given to me.
I am not my own. I have been bought with a price.

I want to honor You with my body.
Therefore, I now offer my body as a living sacrifice to You.

[Begin your body scan. Start with your left foot and leg as you imagine a scanner passing over it from bottom to top. Pause at various places to feel any sensation, no sensation, or sensations that come and go. Focus your attention on that part of your body. Notice how sensations may change. Thank God for that part of your body. Be creative in what you thank Him for. You may thank Him for how your knee flexes, for your kneecap, or for the cartilage and ligaments that hold your knee together.

Now move to your right leg and do the same, noticing sensations that come and go. Thank God at various places on your leg.

Move to your torso and then up your left hand and arm and up your right hand and arm. Thank God at various places in your torso and hands and arms.

Now move up your neck, up your face, and finally up through your head. You may thank Him for things that seem insignificant, such as your eyelashes or the contours of your ear. Remember, God has fashioned you as the crown of His creation.

Simply notice and express thanks. You are here to be with your body in the presence of the One who created it. Sometimes you may want to revisit your anchor verses during your body scan. That's fine. When your timer sounds, you can stop, even if you haven't scanned your entire body. If you want to, you can keep going after your timer sounds. Close with these prayers.]

Lord, thank You for giving me my body. I am fearfully and
wonderfully made.
I yield it to You today as a living sacrifice.

[end of the practice]

As you become familiar with each practice, it will feel less awkward. You'll naturally begin to move on to the next letter and practice. The image of the bone scan will prompt you to do the skills for that practice. You may spend more time on the body scan than in other skills in the other practices. But remember, length is not as important as consistency.

So, now we've seen how holy noticing can benefit our bodies. But it can also improve the quality of our relationships. In the next chapter, we'll look at the *R* in the BREATHe model—"Review and Renew Your *Relationships*"—using the concentric circles exercise to improve your ability to intuit the emotions, intentions, and motivations of others.[29]

Chapter Summary

- **Practice One in the BREATHe Model:** *"B:* Ponder and Yield Your *Body."* You learned how to use two skills to reduce the harmful effects on your body from chronic stress, which can hinder your relationship with God.

- **Anchor Verses:** Psalm 139:14; 1 Corinthians 6:19–20 and Romans 12:1

- **Visual Metaphor:** a body scan

- **Skills:** body scan, gratefulness exercises

- **Practice Steps:**

  1) *Formal practice:* During each of the next five days, take three to five minutes once or twice a day to practice the twin skills of the body scan and the gratefulness exercises.

2) *"e: Engage the World like Christ" practice*: To build
   your gratefulness muscles, set a timer on your phone
   to remind you once each hour to pause a few seconds
   to thank God for something you've never thanked
   Him for before.

Bonus material available at www.holynoticing.com/bonus:

• BREATHe Model Practice Outline.

CHAPTER 5

Practice Two: Review and Renew Your Relationships

Empathy is the ability to step outside of your own bubble and into the bubbles of other people.

—C. JOYBELL

CHAPTER BIG IDEA: This chapter unpacks the *R* in the BREATHe model. *R* stands for "Review and Renew Your *Relationships*." You will learn how holy noticing can develop your empathy, sensitivity, and compassion for those in your circle of relationships.

THE DOCTOR'S NEWS WAS GRIM. A rare cancer had caused three golf ball–sized tumors to grow in Eugene's brain. There was no cure, and he had only a few months to live. In his memoir *Chasing Daylight*, published after his death, Eugene O'Kelley describes how he focused on his relationships during his last days. As a successful CEO of a $4 billion accounting firm, he had made his mark in the business world. Yet after receiving his diagnosis, he left the firm within two weeks.

One night as he pondered his remaining time on earth, he sketched five concentric circles as a map of his relationships. He put his family's names in the center circle and the names of other relationships in the outer circles. That night he committed to systematically spend quality time with each of these people, especially those in the inner circle.

As I read this sobering story, I recalled attending an evangelism class taught by Dr. Oscar Thompson during my seminary days. He was also battling cancer, and he taught a similar concept he called *concentric circles of concern*,[1] a way to think about those we know who need to hear the gospel.

In this chapter, you'll use the *concentric circles* concept as a key holy-noticing skill to help enhance your relationships. Although you'll learn the skill in your private devotions, this practice will yield benefits in your daily life.

As we grow into adulthood, we often develop unhealthy relationship patterns. Many times, these patterns are rooted in our childhood experiences. Psychologists use the term *attachment* to describe the degree to which we feel secure, loved, and connected to others. Recent discoveries show that if we felt loved and securely attached to our parents as infants, we'll most likely develop healthy relationship patterns as adults. If we didn't, we've probably unconsciously developed unhealthy ways of relating to others. Research has shown, though, that a mindful lifestyle can improve our relationships[2] by helping us become less self-focused.

How Holy Noticing Improves Our Relationships

Holy noticing helps us be more present with others.

Have you ever talked with someone and then noticed that they hadn't heard a thing you said? Or has your mind ever wandered in the middle of a conversation, as you rehearse what you plan to say in response? When you tuned back into the conversation, maybe you realized you had no idea what was just said. That has happened to me, and it's quite embarrassing.

> **Rather than rehearsing what we want to say next, this practice helps us suspend our automatic responses in favor of being present so others feel fully heard.**

A part of our brain activates when we're thinking about ourselves or what others may be thinking about us.[3] When that happens, we aren't truly present for others. Perhaps that is why James instructs us to "be quick to listen, slow to speak" (1:19).

Holy noticing helps quiet this circuit,[4] which in turn helps us be more present with others. Rather than rehearsing what we want to say next, this practice helps us suspend our automatic responses in favor of being present so others feel fully heard. Tricia McCary Rhodes writes, "As we develop the discipline of *presence*, we begin to honor and attend to the people around us, opening ourselves up to the wonder of *koinonia*, the building of spiritual community."[5]

Holy noticing helps us tune into others better.

The flip side of self-centeredness is "others-centeredness." The apostle Paul wrote, "In humility value others above yourselves, not looking to your own interests but each of you to the interests of others" (Phil. 2:4). And others-centeredness is deeply rooted in how our brains process our thoughts and interactions.

In Italy in the 1960s, neuroscientists accidentally discovered something interesting that they later called *mirror neurons*. In their lab, they noticed that when a monkey reached for a peanut, specific neurons in the monkey's brain would fire. But they also discovered that those same neurons fired when the monkey simply *observed* the researchers reach for a peanut. In other words, the monkey's brain reacted in the same way whether it had actually reached for the food or was merely observing the behavior of the researchers. Thus these neurons, also discovered in human brains, got the name *mirror* neurons.[6]

These same brain cells affect our relationships. They form part of a brain circuit[7] that helps us relationally resonate with people.[8] We sense the emotions of others, and at the same time, we feel those same emotions in ourselves. It's like when someone tears up as they share a personal story, we also tend to tear up as we feel their emotion.

Holy noticing engages mirror neurons[9] by helping us take the focus off ourselves, thereby improving our ability to pay attention to the nonverbal body nuances and facial cues in others while at the same time decreasing own emotional biases.[10] We read between the lines better.[11] We see things more as they are and tune in better to the needs of others.[12] Of course, an over- or under-sensitive mind can certainly misconstrue these subtle signals, so be sure to practice good communication skills so that you can confirm (or deny) what you are sensing between the lines.

A holy-noticing lifestyle helps us, under the guidance of the Holy Spirit, be better noticers as we more accurately sense other people's inner world.[13]

Holy noticing increases our empathy for others.

Empathy includes three components: (1) understanding the thoughts of others, (2) feeling the emotions of others, and (3) acting to help others in need. The Bible commands us to show empathy in Romans 12:15: "Rejoice with those who rejoice; mourn with those who mourn." And the Scriptures repeatedly command us to help others in need, such as the poor, orphans, and widows, which involves the acting component of empathy.

Like a neural alarm, holy noticing activates our empathy circuits and creates a compassion brain wave[14] that motivates us to help alleviate suffering.[15] People with such a lifestyle[16] are described as warm and in touch with the sufferings and joys of others.[17]

Sometimes we can become overwhelmed with other people's suffering. One study, however, found that practices in holy noticing not only created more compassion for hurting people but also generated positive feelings and more resilience needed to be able to respond to those needs.[18] Empathy even releases several feel-good brain chemicals,[19] which makes empathy a pleasurable experience we want to repeat.[20]

A mindful lifestyle, rather than being self-indulgent, makes us more sensitive to the emotions and pain of others and increases the likelihood we will do something to relieve their suffering.

Holy noticing increases overall relationship satisfaction.

This lifestyle develops more satisfying relationships[21] as it fosters greater flexibility when we must deal with friction in those relationships.[22] Even just a few minutes of daily practice can enhance temporary mood and improve social connection.[23] When couples apply it to relationships, it increases empathy toward each other,[24] lowers stress brought on by conflict,[25] and makes them less liable to withdraw in times of conflict.[26] Again, remember that the Holy Spirit is the ultimate change agent, and science only confirms how spiritual disciplines affect us.

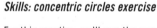

The Holy Spirit is the ultimate change agent, and science only confirms how spiritual disciplines affect us.

One expert believes that one of our human senses is relational, a sense that makes us feel connected to others.[27] He describes it as "being felt" by others, what the Bible calls community (see Acts 2:42–47). Holy noticing enhances skills that foster community.

Formal Practice > R:
Review and Renew Your Relationships
Anchor verse: John 13:34–35

Skills: concentric circles exercise

For this practice, we'll use the concentric circles concept I mentioned in the chapter opening. The concentric circles exercise is a visual way to inventory the health of your relationships. As you prepare to practice this skill, envision who you might place in the inner circle (perhaps family members and close friends). Then envision who you might put in the next few circles (perhaps work associates, neighbors, or extended family). You can fill in the concentric circles diagram below if that helps you with these names.]

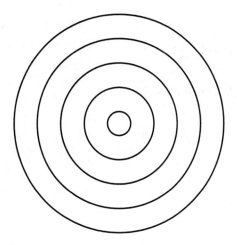

You'll begin by thinking of someone in your inner circle and asking yourself questions such as: "How are things in my relationship with this individual?" "Is our relationship healthy?" "Is there some work I need to do?" "Is there something I should be praying for in this relationship?" Then make your way through as many other names in the inner and outer circles as possible. I usually spend the most time in the inner circle unless something is amiss in a relationship in one of the outer circles.

If a difficult person comes to mind during this exercise, lovingly bring them before God. Hold them before Him with openhearted, non-judgmental, loving attention. Pray for God to show them His love. Pray that God would increase your love for them. Pray that He would show you how to act when you're around them. As you do this, you will become more inclined to favorably respond to them the next time you meet.

Your mind may wander into imaginary scenarios and arguments with that person, creating thoughts fraught with emotion, innuendo, assumptions, and bad attitudes. Try to catch yourself when that happens. Confess any sinful attitudes. The longer you mentally role-play these conversations and arguments, the more your stress-response accelerator will engage and stir up anxious and angry feelings.

In chapter 8 you'll learn a skill to combat those afflictive emotions.

Until then you might want to meditate on Zechariah 7:10, which has helped me combat such thoughts: "Do not plot evil against each other."

As you learn the *R* practice of holy noticing, make space for God to expand your perspective toward difficult people. Try to see them from His viewpoint, through the eyes of grace. One expert[28] tries to visualize that difficult person in his life (if an adult) as a tender five-year-old who was mistreated and unloved as a child. As a result, they've brought unhealthy emotional baggage into their adulthood that has contributed to his tension with them. As he views them in that way, he sees them as a larger version of that hurting child. This perspective can give you a more grace-filled perspective and foster compassion toward difficult people.

However, if you get stuck in your thoughts and emotions with a difficult person, try to move on to another practice, perhaps even back to "*B*: Ponder and Yield Your *Body*." Over time, as you practice "*R*: Review and Renew Your *Relationships*," God's Spirit will change your heart toward these individuals. You may need to build up slowly. Eventually you will become more disposed to think of them through the eyes of grace.

Sit in a comfortable chair, in a place free from distraction. I've written in *italics* what you may *think*, *verbalize*, or *pray* during the practice session, and I put in [brackets] my comments and suggestions. In this example, I have inserted my breath prayers as well as other personal components as if I were doing it.

Now you are ready. Get comfortable, start your timer for three minutes (or six if you are combining *B* and *R*), and close your eyes to visually block distractions.

Review and Renew Your *Relationships*—Practice

[Begin with long, slow breaths.
Breathe in.
Breathe out.

Breathe in.
Breathe out.
Breathe in and breathe out with your breath prayer]

Holy Spirit [the in-breath]
Breath on me [the out-breath]

[Repeat your breath prayer as long as you want. You may want to include other breath prayers, such as *Lord Jesus* (on the in-breath) *You are good* (on the out-breath).]
[Move on to your anchor verses. Meditate on them by reading or reciting them from memory.]

Lord, I bring my relationships before You. I want to review and
renew them as Your Spirit guides.
Please give me a sense of Your grace right now.
Show me Your love.
Help me love others as You have loved me.

[Now visualize those in your concentric circles. Start in the center circle with those closest to you. Ask questions like the ones I mentioned above.]

How are things in this relationship?
Is this relationship healthy?
Is there some work I need to do?
Is there something regarding this relationship I should be
praying about?
Do I need to confess a bad attitude toward this person?

[Linger a bit with the image of that person in your mind. Pray for them as the Spirit prompts. Then move to the next person in your concentric circles diagram, and so on. Don't feel as though you need to cover every relationship. God will bring to mind those you need to focus on today. If you get stuck on a person who invokes a negative response, move on. The deeper the hurt, the longer it will take to heal and wish this person well. When your timer sounds, you can stop, even if you haven't covered all the relationships in your concentric circles. That's okay. If you want to, you can continue after your timer sounds. You're in no rush. Close your session with these prayers.]

Lord, thank You for putting these people in my circle of relationships.
I recommit them to You.
Help me refresh and renew these relationships on an ongoing basis.
If I must interact with a difficult person today, give me Your grace to respond in a godly way.

[end of the practice]

By now you've experienced the first two practices and hopefully you are doing them in the same session, one after the other. If you are combining two or more practices, you don't necessarily need to repeat your slow breathing and breath prayer with each of the practices. Do it once as you begin with "B." However, when your mind wanders, it's best to go back to your breath and then return to the current practice. Thank God for helping you realize when your mind has wandered. Spell out BREATHe until you get to the letter where you left off, do a few breath prayers, and start again.

One final reminder. During the day, you may encounter or interact with one of the difficult people in your concentric circles. When you anticipate this, your mind may tend to dredge up past memories and experiences and project them into the future, assuming the same difficulties will repeat themselves. Fearful foreboding will color your experience and hinder you from being mindfully present in the moment.

If you practice holy noticing in those moments, you can turn down your brain's anxiety centers and see reality as it is, without bringing unhealthy commentary or needless emotion to the encounter. At such moments, practice the *E* of the BREATHe model, "Notice and Engage Your *Environment*," to bring your mind back to the present moment. In the next chapter, you'll learn how to do this *E* practice and how it can improve your ability to pay attention and be more fully present in the moment.

Chapter Summary

- **Practice Two in the BREATHe Model:** "*R*: Review and Renew Your *Relationships*." You learned how holy noticing can develop your empathy, sensitivity, and compassion for those in your circle of relationships.

- **Anchor Verses:** John 13:34–35

- **Visual Metaphor:** concentric circles

- **Skills:** concentric circles exercise

- **Practice Steps:**

    1) *Formal practice*: During each of the next five days, add this practice to the *B* practice and take six minutes to practice both "*B*: Ponder and Yield Your *Body*" (use the body scan, gratefulness exercises); and "*R*: Review and Renew Your *Relationships*" (use the concentric circles exercise).

2) *"e: Engage the World like Christ" practice*: For five of
the next seven days, send an email, text, or a personal
note to someone to encourage them.

Bonus material available at www.holynoticing.com/bonus:
Concentric Circles Diagram.

CHAPTER 6

Practice Three: Notice and Engage Your Environment

Distraction is the primary spiritual problem in our day.
—RICHARD J. FOSTER

The faculty of voluntarily bringing back a wandering attention, over and over again, is the very root of judgment, character, and will.
—WILLIAM JAMES

CHAPTER BIG IDEA: This chapter unpacks the *E* in the BREATHe model. *E* stands for "Notice and Engage Your *Environment* (your current surroundings)." In this chapter, you will learn a practice that will help you focus, sustain, and improve your ability to pay attention to what's happening around you.

WE LIVE IN AN AGE OF PERPETUAL DISTRACTION. As I write this chapter, I'm battling it while sitting in a McDonald's restaurant. To my left, a wall-mounted TV announces the latest picks in the NFL draft. Michael Jackson's song "Thriller" is blasting through the restaurant's speakers right above me. My iPhone lies in front of my computer, reminding me that a text or call may arrive any second. This culture of distraction has resulted in something called continuous partial attention, which means "to keep a top-level item in focus, and constantly scan the periphery in case something more important emerges."[1]

The rise of the internet and 24-7 connectivity has fueled distraction. Teens and adults in the US now pick up their smartphones every 4.3 minutes,[2] and 62 percent of smartphone users grab their phones as soon as they wake up.[3] One psychologist aptly captures our information overload world by calling the World Wide Web (WWW) "Whatever, Whenever, Wherever."[4]

Not surprisingly, our ability to pay attention has dropped in recent years. In fact, one popular urban legend says that we now can pay attention for only about eight seconds on average before getting distracted, which is less than a goldfish.[5] They beat us humans by a second. Although that might not have a lot of scientific proof, it illustrates how attention is scattered in today's world. And when we're online, the duration of time between focusing on an online task and attending to an offline distraction has dropped from an average of once every three minutes to an average of once every forty-five seconds.[6]

Author-pastor Tim Keller was asked why people struggle to connect with God. He wrote, "Noise and distraction. It's easier to tweet than pray."[7] The flip side of that question points to the key skill that helps us stay spiritually healthy: distraction management, or getting better at paying attention.[8]

I was a test subject in an often-used experiment as I was completing my executive master's degree in the neuroscience of leadership. In one of our online sessions, the professor told us she was going to show us a video and assign us a task that most students failed. She said although most of us would not get the correct answer, we should still try our best.

Her prediction aroused my competitive spirit, and I vowed to prove her wrong. She instructed us to watch a short video of several college students passing a basketball to one another. Our assignment? Count the number of passes. Then she played the video.

As it played, I scrutinized every student and every pass. I counted sixteen passes. After about ninety seconds, the video ended. She asked us how many we counted. Only two of us got the right answer. I felt quite proud that I had proved her wrong.

Then she asked, "Did you see it?"

What? I didn't know what she meant.

"Did you see the gorilla?"

I responded, "There was no gorilla."

In the moment I was thinking, *That comment doesn't make any sense. I wonder if something is wrong with her brain.* (She was a neuroscientist.)

She said, "I'm going to play the video again. Watch for the gorilla. Ignore the passes this time."

She began the video and just as she said, about thirty seconds in, a person dressed in a gorilla suit walked in front of the students passing the ball, waved at the camera, and then walked out of view of the camera.

I felt a bit embarrassed because I thought something was wrong with *her* brain. Almost every student in that class had also missed the gorilla.

What happened? I had focused so intently on one thing that I missed something obvious, the gorilla in the room. Surprisingly, 50 percent of people who participate in this experiment miss the gorilla as well, which illustrates how distraction often makes us miss what is right in front of us.

A lifestyle of holy noticing, however, can help us pay better attention in our relationships, our work life, and in our spiritual disciplines such as prayer and Bible reading. This chapter's practice, the *E* in the BREATHe model, "Notice and Engage Your *Environment*," will hone those attentional skills.

Attentiveness in Scripture

Scripture devotes a great deal to the topic of attention. The New Testament writers use the Greek word for attention, *prosecho*, several times (e.g., 2 Peter 1:19). The writer of Hebrews uses the word when he admonishes us to "pay the most careful attention" to the prophets and the words of Jesus (Heb. 2:1). The word literally means to "turn your mind toward something."

> **The Bible instructs us to focus our attention on God, His works, and His deeds (see Josh. 1:8; Heb. 12:2; Phil. 4:8).**

The Bible instructs us to focus our attention on God, His works, and His deeds (see Josh. 1:8; Heb. 12:2; Phil. 4:8). It commands us to continually meditate on and pay attention to His Word so that we obey its precepts (see Josh. 1:8–9; Ps. 1:2). Moses would have missed God's call on his life had he not paid attention to the burning bush (Exod. 3). Samuel would have missed his calling as a prophet had he not learned to pay attention to the voice of God at a very early age (1 Sam. 3).

The apostle Paul addresses distraction in the context of marriage in 1 Corinthians 7 when he reminds believers to be watchful for and attentive to Jesus' pending return. When Peter preached and worked miracles in Samaria, his audience "paid close attention to what he said" (Acts 8:6, 10). Peter admonishes us to "pay attention" to the truth of the gospel as well (2 Peter 1:19).

After God brought the Israelites through the Red Sea, they began to grumble against Moses's leadership. God then issued a test about where they should direct their attention. He told Moses to tell the people: "If you listen carefully to the LORD your God and do what is right in his eyes, if you *pay attention* to his commands and keep all his decrees, I will not bring on you any of the diseases I brought on the Egyptians, for I am the LORD, who heals you" (Ex. 15:26, emphasis mine).

As King David gave his attention to creation, he was struck by God's detailed care for us and penned these words:

> When I look at your heavens, the work of your fingers,
>> the moon and the stars, which you have set in place,
> what is man that you are mindful of him,
>> and the son of man that you care for him?
> (Ps. 8:3–4 ESV)

The New Testament warns us six times how unchecked distraction affects our soul, summarized by three outcomes: it blinds our souls to God, closes off community with Him, and mutes the urgency of God.[9]

Unfortunately, paying attention is not automatic. Jesus knew this and often said, "He who has ears to hear, let him hear" (Matt. 11:15, Mark 4:9 ESV). He wasn't contrasting those who had physical ears to someone who might not. Rather, He was challenging His hearer to truly pay attention to what He was saying.

Attention and Mind Wandering

There are two kinds of attention: *narrow* (think of a bird eating birdseed from one of the feeders on our deck) and *broad* (that same bird keeping a lookout for our Yorkshire terrier, Sammy, who loves to chase him).[10] Attention also involves specific brain chemicals in three phases—alert, attend, and focus. We can understand these phases by breaking down how a professional photographer might take a picture.[11]

A photographer first points his camera at the object. Likewise, in the first phase of attention, something *alerts* you, such as the bing of a text message. Next, the photographer zooms in. In the second phase of attention, you *attend* to an object such as your iPhone. Finally, the photographer sharpens the camera's focus. In the final phase of attention, you *focus* on the object and read the text. Attention is not easy to maintain,[12] but practicing holy noticing can grow your attentional muscles. Each time you redirect your attention from a distraction, you flex and strengthen those attentional muscles.[13]

Also, the more you sustain your attention to something and then repeat it, a concept called *attention density* deepens what you pay attention to. Sustained attention increases the likelihood that a habit, value, or belief gets more deeply wired into your brain. Christian neuroscientist Dr. Jeffrey Schwartz writes, "In the brain, attention density is the first—and most important—step in creating strong, enduring brain circuits. Attention density . . . causes focused attention to have powerful effects on the brain by activating Hebb's law."[14] Hebb's law states that that brain circuits that fire together, wire together.

For example, each time you stop yourself from mind wandering in your daily practice, you strengthen neural pathways that help build your attention through four microskills.[15] First, you notice that your attention is not where it needs to be (noticing). Second, you move your attention from the distraction, whether it's plans for dinner, the argument you had with your

child, or a looming work deadline (shifting). Third, you direct
your attention back to the component of the BREATHe model
(focusing). Fourth, you keep your attention there (sustained
attention). You will gradually build your attentional muscles,
which will result in the steadfast mind Isaiah wrote about: "You
will keep in perfect peace those whose minds are steadfast,
because they trust in you" (Isa. 26:3). *Steadfast* means "to rely
on" or "sustain." So when we train our minds to be attentive,
as we trust the Lord, we are led to experience His sustained
peace or *shalom*.

When I began to learn about and practice the art of holy
noticing, I'd get angry when my mind wandered from where I
wanted it to be (focused on the Lord) to something else (what I
wanted for breakfast). When that happened, I needlessly wasted
my emotional energy. Although I still occasionally get frustrated,
I'm learning to be easier on myself and appreciate my growing
ability to catch myself when my mind does wander. My inner
dialogue is now, *Oh, my mind wandered again. Thanks, Lord,
for reminding me. Now, where was I?* B . . . R . . . *oh yeah, on* E.

Sometimes, however, the Holy Spirit may lead our minds
to wander for a good purpose. Author Drew Dyck makes this
interesting observation about beneficial mind wandering:

> I also picked up a helpful tip for what to do with my wan-
> dering mind. It came from German theologian and Nazi
> resister Dietrich Bonhoeffer. During WWII, Hitler closed
> all the seminaries, so Bonhoeffer ran a secret underground
> seminary for a small group of men. Bonhoeffer required
> his students to meditate for two hours each day on a pas-
> sage of Scripture. But the students were struggling. They
> came to Bonhoeffer and complained that their minds kept

wandering away from the text and back to the troubles at home. "Follow your mind where it goes," Bonhoeffer told them. "Follow it until it stops, and then, wherever it stops, make that person or problem, a matter for prayer."

I found this strategy liberating. Rather than feeling bad about my wandering mind, or even trying to rein it in—I could follow it. And when I did, I realized Bonhoeffer was right. It often led to people or problems, which I could pray about. It turned out to be a great way to find worthwhile topics to bring to God. Maybe my wandering mind isn't so bad after all.[16]

How Holy Noticing Improves Attention

It helps us appreciate the familiar.

Habituation is a term that describes how we tune out the familiar to conserve our mental resources. We usually notice something new, novel, or unexpected just long enough to determine if it's a threat or not (e.g., a loud sound at night). Once we know it's not a threat (a dish fell off the counter), we tune it out. Habituation happens, however, to almost everything. We no longer notice the pictures on our walls, the dead bush in the yard, the flowers in the flower bed, or even distress in a family member. We can even become habituated to God's Word, church, and our relationship to Jesus. We simply get accustomed to these relationships and experiences when they become commonplace and frequent.

However, when we more deeply pay attention to the familiar, the commonplace can become fresh and interesting again. Noticing and engaging our environment can help make that happen.

It keeps us from missing what is right under our noses.[17]

Remember how I missed the gorilla in the room in the video? That *miss* was inconsequential. But it's not so inconsequential when we miss important nonverbal cues from those we love (like when my wife is hurting, and I miss it from her tone of voice) or miss the promptings of the Holy Spirit because we weren't paying attention (like when I should stop and talk to a homeless person instead of passing him by). This practice helps make us more adept "noticers" because we learn to direct our attentional resources to the truly important. We become more alert to subtle yet important experiences and environmental cues. One study showed that even a session as short as seventeen minutes helps us be better noticers.[18]

It enhances working memory.

Working memory is like a mental chalkboard where we store temporary items in our mind (like a phone number) until they move to long-term memory, we no longer need them, or they get "erased" because new information takes up space there. A lifestyle of holy noticing can enhance this crucial kind of memory.[19]

It helps us avoid multitasking and its cost.

Our minds can focus only on one task at a time that requires direct attention. We fool ourselves by thinking we can perform two tasks at once that require our attention, such as when I try listening to my wife on the phone and trying to (very quietly) type out an email. I've gotten busted a few times for attempting that stunt. Actually, when we try this, we're simply switching our attention back and forth between two tasks and becoming less efficient and less effective in both. Holy noticing makes us more aware of multitasking and the cost from this constant switching.[20] It helps us become more aware of our unawareness and thus helps us stay on task more easily.

It can help us grow spiritually.

Has your mind ever wandered while praying? Mine has. University professor Martin Laird writes, "Prayer consists of attention," and "the quality of the attention counts for much in the quality of the prayer."[21] And since holy noticing helps build our attentional muscles, it can help improve our prayer lives because our minds wander less.

It counters autopilot mode.

In one often-repeated study, the door study,[22] strangers on a street are asked for directions by an experimenter involved in the study (the stranger is unaware of the study). As he gives directions, two people carrying a door rudely barge between the two of them, temporarily blocking the stranger's view of the experimenter. Unbeknownst to the one giving directions, someone else replaces the original "asker" while the original one moves away, hidden by the moving door. The new person wears different clothes and sometimes is even a different gender. Surprisingly, only 50 percent of the people noticed that a new person was now standing there.

These experiences occur when we get into autopilot mode, acting without thinking, which prevents us from being fully aware of what's happening around us. When autopilot drives us, we temporarily lose our holy-noticing ability, unable to pay attention in the present moment. The skill you'll learn in this practice helps develop attention to the here and now. As you learn to focus longer on things around you that you normally would ignore (such as familiar sights and sounds), you'll enhance your attention skills.[23] This skill of paying attention to what your senses tell you about your environment can transfer to improved attention to biblical truth. And as those truths get embedded more deeply in your mind, they can change behavior.[24]

Charles Spurgeon even taught his students to pay attention to their environment:

> Charles encouraged his students that if they kept their eyes open that they would "not see even a dog following his master, nor a mouse peeping up from his hole, nor will you hear even a gentle scratching behind the wainscot, without getting something to weave into your sermons if your faculties are alert."[25]

Formal Practice > *E*: Notice and Engage Your *Environment*

In this practice you will learn to hone your noticing ability by attending more directly to your senses. Again, recall that holy noticing is an art.

Although this practice in the BREATHe model focuses on sight and sound, this skill can involve all your senses. It might mean listening more deeply to the sounds around you during your devotional time. It might involve noticing something new about the flowers in the potted plant on the windowsill. It might include paying more attention to how the cover of your Bible feels, to the texture of its onion-skin paper,

Most importantly, this skill can help you notice people around you with whom you need to connect.

or to a fresh insight from Scripture as you read it. You may even give greater attention to faint smells you've taken for granted—the smell of morning coffee or the crispness of a fall morning. You can even apply this skill to your sense of taste—more deeply noticing your bagel's nutty flavor or the soft, sweet taste a bite of banana leaves on your tongue. And, most importantly, it can help you notice people around you with whom you need to connect.

As you are now using several of the practices together, you may find it helpful to download the BREATHe Model Practice Outline chart at www .holynoticing.com/bonus to guide you.

Anchor Verses: Psalm 95:4–5; Psalm 8

Skills: deep listening, focused observation exercises

I enjoy WWII submarine movies, and especially enjoy scenes where a sub is trying to elude a ship on the surface. In these scenes, the sub's crew goes deathly silent as an enemy destroyer lurks above it to drop depth charges in attempts to destroy it. The crew hears the unnerving *ping . . . ping . . . ping* as the sonar sound hits the sub's hull. This image helps me remember this practice as I mentally ping my environment for sounds (and sights) upon which to focus my attention.

This next component of the BREATHe model may seem a bit odd and difficult in the beginning. However, it has become one of the most helpful ways, in the moment, to keep my mind from wandering into negative territory. By deliberately practicing *noticing and engaging your environment* through paying attention to the sights and sounds around you, you will grow your attentional skills. As a result, you will more consistently attend to your relationships, redirect negative thinking, and catch and stop mind wandering in your devotional life. It's actually an application of the adage "Stop and smell the roses."

For this skill, I suggest you start with deep listening (to sounds) and then trying focused observation (to sights). With deep listening, keep your eyes closed. This minimizes mind wandering since you can't see items around you that could be a distraction. You'll simply listen to the sounds around you, in front or behind, to the sides, or those above or below. When I do my morning practice, sometimes I turn on either a small heater or a fan, depending on the time of the year. I listen for the pitch, tone, and timber of the fan, the air-conditioning, clocks, and even the tinnitus in my ears. I avoid attaching meaning or narrative to them, even to sounds I may not enjoy, such as a neighbor dog's incessant yelping.

I simply listen.

When I start to add commentary to those sounds, I try to notice it and then bring my attention back to the sounds themselves. I sometimes imagine that I am hearing them for the first time, as if each sound is brand new to me. I try to distinguish sounds within sounds, such as the *hummmm* coming the heater's fan from the *shhhhhhh* sound of the air blowing through the heater's grid. I sometimes try to notice the spaces between sounds (i.e., the spaces between the *tick* and *tock* of the clock).

Sit in a comfortable chair, in a place free from distraction. I've written in *italics* what you may *think*, *verbalize*, or *pray* during the practice session, and I put in [brackets] my comments and suggestions. In this example I will insert my breath prayers as well as other personal components as if I were doing it myself.

Now you are ready. Get comfortable, start your timer for three minutes (or nine minutes if you are combining *B*, *R*, and *E*), and close your eyes to visually block distractions. If you're moving on to *E* from *B* and *R*, there is no need to start by focusing on your breath.

Again, developing this component of the BREATHe model will help you pay better attention to daily situations. For example, I write my books each Friday in a local McDonald's. After I place my lunch order, sometimes I have to wait a few minutes to get my food. Often during those few minutes, I will simply focus on and listen to the sounds around me (beeps, buzzes, and the hum of converstions) to counter my mind's tendency to wander into negative thinking.

At other times, I'll focus on some visual aspect of God's handiwork, which helps me apply what Paul admonished us to do in Philippians 4:8. In that verse, after he lists several positive qualities, he then says we are to "think about such things." As you learn this skill, you'll discover many of your own personal applications.

Notice and Engage Your *Environment*—Practice

[Begin with long, slow breaths.
Breathe in.
Breathe out.
Breathe in.
Breathe out.
Breathe in and breathe out with your breath prayer.]

Holy Spirit [the in-breath]
Breathe on me [the out-breath]

[Repeat your breath prayer as long as you want. You may want to include other breath prayers such as *Lord Jesus* (on the in-breath) *You are good* (on the out-breath).]
[Move on to your anchor verses. Meditate on them by reading or reciting them from memory.]

Lord, I bring my attention to the environment You have placed me in right now.
Thank You
. . . for the ability to hear
. . . for the air I breathe

. . . for Your magnificent creation
. . . for the sounds that surround me right now.

[Imagine you are sending a sonar "ping" into your surroundings. Listen deeply to the sounds you hear. Is it the air-conditioning, the clock, the wind outside (or the wind blowing in the trees if you are outside), birds chirping, a neighbor's lawn mower, stirrings of your family members in your home?

Listen for whatever comes your way.

Catch yourself if you begin to add commentary, and refocus on the sound.

Just listen to the tone, timber, beat, and so on of the sounds. Remember, you are strengthening your attentional muscles with this skill.

You may want to then try focused observation.

Open your eyes and focus on an object you've not focused on before, such as the flower in the windowsill, the lampshade, the sofa, familiar objects you may have taken for granted. What new things do you notice that you've never seen before? Is it a color, a pattern, or an unusual aspect of that object?

If you are at a window or outside, focus your attention on a tree branch, a leaf, a flower petal, or something else in nature. Notice its shape, color, size, uniqueness, symmetry or asymmetry.

Revel in God's creation.

Remember, you are simply noticing, not adding commentary.]

Lord, I thank You for the senses You've given me to enjoy
Your creation.
Hone my attentional skills.
Help me become a better "holy noticer" of You, Your creation,
and others.

[end of the practice]

So by now you've tried the first three practices (*B*, *R*, and *E*). At this point in your formal practice, try to do all three together, letting one practice flow into the next. The more you practice, the easier it becomes. You don't need to repeat your breath prayers between each practice, unless you mind wanders and it helps to take a few breaths and then spell the word *BREATHe* to get you back to where you left off before your mind wandered.

I enjoy doing this practice outside. We have a swing in our backyard where I sit in the summer for my morning devotions. When I do *E*, I will often direct my "ping" to my left and listen to sounds coming from that direction, such as the rustling of leaves or the sounds of birds. After a minute or two, I direct my hearing forward for a minute or two and then to the right. When I do this outside, it creates a deepening appreciation for God's creation.

The first three practices may give rise to emotions, both pleasant and unpleasant. What do you do with those emotions during your formal practice? In the next practice, *A*, you'll learn how how to deal with them through labeling and releasing your *afflictive* emotions.

Chapter Summary

- **Practice Three in the BREATHe Model:** "*E*: Notice and Engage Your *Environment*." You learned how holy noticing can help you focus, sustain, and improve your ability to pay attention to what's happening around you.

- **Anchor Verses:** Psalm 95:4–5; Psalm 8

- **Visual Metaphor:** sonar
- **Skills:** deep listening, focused observation exercises
- **Practice Steps:**

  1) *Formal practice*: During each of the next five days, add this practice to the *B* and *R* practices and take about ten minutes to practice all three—"*B*: Ponder and Yield Your *Body*" (use the body scan, gratefulness exercises); "*R*: Review and Renew Your *Relationships*" (use the concentric circles exercise); and "*E:* Notice and Engage Your *Environment*" (use the deep listening, focused observation exercises).

  2) *"e: Engage the World like Christ" practice*: Schedule a walk in a natural area this week, perhaps on a walking path along a body of water or in a forest. As you slowly walk, deeply notice God's handiwork. Pause often to worship Him for His handiwork, thanking Him for blessing us with the beauty of His creation.

PART 3

"LOOKING IN": OUR INNER WORLD OF THOUGHTS AND FEELINGS

CHAPTER 7

Practice Four: Label and Release Your Afflictive Emotions (Affect)

Let us keep our eyes always fixed on the depths
of our heart with an unceasing mindfulness of God.
—BISHOP DIADOCHUS OF PHOTIKE

CHAPTER BIG IDEA: This chapter unpacks the *A* in the BREATHe model. *A* stands for "Label and Release Your *Afflictive* Emotions." Another word that fits *A* that I will interchange with afflictive emotions is *affect*, a comprehensive term that describes our emotions, disposition, and affections. In this chapter you will learn how to label and release your afflictive emotions to the Lord.

WHEN OUR KIDS WERE YOUNG, we took an annual vacation to Mississippi, where my wife's parents lived. Free babysitting, free food, and free lodging for a week was a dream come true for a family with three preschoolers.

Not only did my wife's parents frequently take care of the kids, but my father-in-law paid for all-you-can eat buffets, gave us money to go on dates and a shopping spree at the local mall for my wife. He also gave each of our two older kids a roll of quarters to spend at the mall's arcade.

While Mario Bros. and Pac-Man mesmerized my son, Josh, for hours, I would occasionally ask him for a quarter so I could play my favorite game, Whac-A-Mole. It's not a video game, but I think it's a lot more fun. The game console includes a soft hammer and several holes where small mechanical moles randomly pop up and down. The goal is to whack them back into their holes with the hammer before they pop back in themselves. Whac-A-Mole could mesmerize me for hours (well, maybe just a few minutes). Each time I whacked a mole back into its hole, a small paper ticket would spit out of a slot on the side of the machine. I could then redeem the tickets for really cool prizes such as small plastic soldiers with tiny parachutes or Chinese finger puzzles. I usually (and reluctantly) gave my tickets to my son. But I'd convince him how much fun *he* would have if he picked the soldier or the finger trap.

Often we deal with unpleasant emotions in the same way we hit those moles in Whac-A-Mole. We try to whack them away by denying, repressing, or ignoring them. Or we try to manipulate spiritual disciplines to whack them away. If anger pops up, whack it with a prayer. When worry appears, whack it with a Scripture verse. As fear rises up, whack it with an "I rebuke you, Satan" response. Keep in mind that such practices can foster spiritual growth (and holy noticing) when appropriately used.

The problem with the Whac-A-Mole method—which I've often tried—is that it is not an effective way to deal with ongoing negative emotions when used mechanically. Unfortunately, we sometimes view the Bible and prayer as a vending machine. In a similar fashion, we can wrongly assume that reciting the correct verse or praying the right prayer will magically make the difficult emotion disappear. I found that when I tried to use spiritual tools as if they were a formula that guaranteed a particular outcome, although that emotion might subside a bit, it often returned even stronger.

So what do we do with our difficult and afflictive emotions? First, we must appreciate that God gave us a wide range of them. Without emotions, life would be dull. Although psychologists and scientists have created varying lists of them, the most common list includes these eight: fear (and the related emotions anxiety and worry), anger, sadness/depression, disgust, joy/happiness, surprise, trust, and anticipation. And the more we set our minds on wholesome thoughts, the more we will experience these positive emotions (more on that in the next chapter).

The negative emotions, such as anger, fear, depression, and anxiety, aren't pleasant. We often treat them as unruly kids and view them as hindrances to living a full life. So, we try to get rid of them. Yet our efforts often fail, causing these difficult emotions to worsen as if we're fighting quicksand yet still sinking deeper. Although we try to ignore, deny, suppress, or spiritualize away our afflictive emotions with the Whac-A-Mole method, we actually strengthen those negative emotions we're trying to remove.[1] We're only able to put a lid on them for a short time, or we make them worse by rehearsing them, ruminating on them, catastrophizing (thinking "the sky is falling"), or judging ourselves. We wonder why we're such bad Christians and tell ourselves that good Christians shouldn't feel this way. This only exacerbates our anger, fear, or depression because it dredges up even more negative feelings. What began as a small issue can snowball into a giant emotional quagmire.

If we were to picture the components of an emotion as a formula, it might look like this: *emotions = thoughts + feelings*

+ *behavioral impulses* + *bodily sensations.*[2] All four of these components act upon one another because an emotion is a bundle of these experiences. When we repeatedly experience the same negative emotions and don't proactively respond to them in a healthy way, neuroplasticity sets in, which is the ability of the brain to change itself in response to internal and external stimuli. Brain networks strengthen around these emotions, thoughts, and responses, making us more inclined to default to them.

This brain effect creates lower thresholds for afflictive emotions because our mind trolls our memory banks to look for reasons why we feel as we do. It dredges up memories to explain why something like this happened in the past or creates scenarios about what might happen in the future. The brain's alarm (the amygdala) magnifies the emotion beyond the current situation by adding memories of past threats to potential future worries. Our brains plunder the past to find new material to add to our current anxiety and fear.

We brood, ruminate, and overthink. We assume that we must remove or escape the pain before we can move forward in life. Our emotional and mental pain becomes part of how we define ourselves and our worth before God. Not only do we reinforce our negative emotions by suppression or denial, but "research has shown that when you suppress thoughts in the presence of an emotion, eventually the emotion evokes the thought, and the suppression strategies evoke both the thought and the emotion."[3]

God gave me clarity and insight into these issues one day as I prepared a sermon. I have often felt strangled by anxiety, which is appropriate given that the old English word for "anxiety" means "to strangle." And I can identify when Proverbs

12:25 says that "anxiety weighs down the heart," since the Hebrew word for "anxiety" means "the emotional distress caused when something vital to your life feels threatened."[4] My anxiety has often strangled out my joy and peace, which we believers are promised in the Bible. And I was puzzled why God didn't answer my prayers to take away my anxiety and replace it with His *shalom*. I wondered if I was doing something wrong.

Over time, I realized I *was* doing something wrong. I often prayed that God would take away my anxiety. Unknowingly, I was asking Him to perform a miracle. God certainly answers prayer and works miracles, and an imbalance in our brain chemistry can foster anxiety disorders. But was it right for me to ask God for a miracle *each time* I felt anxious, without me taking some ownership? It would be akin to a person addicted to cigarettes praying each time they lit up that God would miraculously take away their addiction without recognizing that they have some personal responsibility to make efforts to quit.

Through my attempts to use prayer and Scripture to remove the afflictive emotion of anxiety, I realized I was unconsciously expecting God to suspend His own created laws of nature to supercede the way my body and brain works.

During the first several decades of my life, I really didn't know how to deal with my anxiety, not realizing that my response to it had actually sculpted my brain circuits to be more sensitive to anxiety. By using the Whac-A-Mole method, I had in fact created a strong "anxiety circuit," which probably also involved an imbalance of neurotransmitters (chemical messengers) related to anxiety. Each time I tried to deal with anxiety using these spiritual disciplines as "Band-Aids," I was in effect asking God to miraculously reconfigure my brain to be less anxious, without changing my behavior, thinking patterns, or relationship to my emotions. I was expecting Him to immediately do these things to my brain:

- Purge excess amounts of the stress hormone cortisol from my blood that had built up over time.

- Force the fight-flight center of my brain offline, even though it had been made more sensitive to stress by my thinking.

- Rewire my anxiety circuits, which had been made stronger by my tendency to please people.

- Deactivate my genetic tendency toward anxiety.

- Force my brain's CEO to work against my will to think only positive thoughts.

- Activate my brain cells that release dopamine, one of the feel-good brain chemicals, to give me an extra spritz of it so that I'd feel more peaceful.

And if God did all that, *poof!* . . . my anxiety would instantly disappear. Peace would fill my soul. I would have experienced a miracle.

This insight, that I was expecting God for a miracle each time, helped me think more responsibly about my role to trust Him to help me work within His created laws of body and brain as His Spirit changed me. It reminded me that every answer to prayer does not have to circumvent His natural laws to make it a God thing. This fresh insight motivated me to learn about all these mindful practices and how I could leverage what I was learning about it, while respecting how God designed my brain.

Holy noticing can actually resculpt brain pathways that lower the activity of our brain's anxiety centers.[5] It's a spiritual discipline that helps us step out of the self-reflective, inner chatter mode we're in about half our waking hours.[6] It helps us step back, notice, and be objective in the face of our tendency to default to emotional subjectivity.

Afflictive emotions and mental health issues are looming crises in our world today. Depression is taking a staggering toll on our well-being, and the latest statistics show that 10 percent of the world's population will likely become clinically depressed within a year. It will become the world's second biggest health issue by 2020, surpassing arthritis, heart disease, and many forms of cancer. Depression strikes people of all ages, including kids and teens. It's evil sister, chronic anxiety, is now becoming more common as well. Average levels of anxiety in children and youth are skyrocketing. Depression and anxiety are becoming a scourge today for society in general and Christians in particular,[7] with anxiety disorders affecting approximately forty million adults in the US alone.[8]

The Bible and Our Emotions

The Scriptures don't gloss over our struggle with emotions such as worry, anxiety, fear, and grief. God acknowledges that as created beings we experience a wide range of emotions, some healthy and others not.

The writer of the Old Testament book of Proverbs notes how emotions affect life satisfaction: "A cheerful disposition is good for your health" (Prov. 17:22 MSG); "A happy heart makes the face cheerful, but heartache crushes the spirit" (Prov. 15:13); and, "The human spirit can endure in sickness, but a crushed spirit who can bear?" (Prov. 18:14).

King David becomes agonizingly aware of his emotions as

he felt the pangs of guilt for his affair with Bathsheba and for orchestrating the death of her husband (see 2 Sam. 11).

The apostle Paul intuitively understood how our thoughts and emotions interact, long before neuroscientists discovered it. He understood that we are an integrated body, soul, spirit, and mind, and that thinking influences emotions and vice versa. He counsels us to quickly be aware of our emotions before they turn into sin, writing, "In your anger do not sin" (Eph. 4:26). In the book of Romans, he describes how he wrestled with inner afflictions: "I do not understand what I do. For what I want to do I do not do, but what I hate I do" (Rom. 7:15). Multiple times in the Scriptures he writes about our minds.

Jesus experienced a full range of emotions as well, though He never sinned. He was angry at the money changers in the temple (John 2:13–16) and the disciples who tried to prohibit children from coming to Him (Luke 18:15–17). He was perplexed that only one out of nine lepers thanked Him for healing them (Luke 17:17–19). He wept at learning of Lazarus's death (John 11:35). He agonized in the garden before He was arrested and crucified (Matt. 26:37–44), yet He modeled a calm, dignified mindfulness of His Father's will. And He felt abject loneliness on the cross as He took upon our sins (Matt. 27:33–46).

C. S. Lewis describes Jesus' full range of emotions with these words:

> God could, had He pleased, have been incarnate in a man of iron nerves, the Stoic sort who lets no sigh escape him. Of His great humility He chose to be incarnate in a man of delicate sensibilities, who wept at the grave of Lazarus and sweated blood in Gethsemane. Otherwise we should have

missed the great lesson that it is by *will* alone that a man is good or bad, and that *feelings* are not, in themselves, of any importance. We should also have missed the all-important help of knowing that He has faced all that the weakest of us face.[9]

How Holy Noticing Benefits Our Emotional Lives

In many ways holy noticing decreases the power negative emotions wield over our thinking and behavior.[10] The goal of the holy-noticing lifestyle is not to avoid feelings or to detach ourselves from emotions but to notice and respond to them in a God-honoring way. Some forms of mindfulness do encourage detaching from ourselves—that's not what I'm talking about in this book. One study of nuns who had used a type of holy-noticing prayer for fifteen years revealed that it reduces the activity in our brain's feeler (the amygdala).[11] The practice also lowers anxiety and depression[12] and helps us reduce aggressiveness and anger.[13]

It can help us get unstuck from the automatic responses to our emotions such as reactivity, hopeless thinking, defensiveness, and self-condemning thoughts, including the misconception that good Christians don't feel these kinds of emotions. It can help us develop a window of tolerance, the increasing capacity to "maintain equilibrium in the face of stresses that would once have thrown us off kilter."[14]

> **The goal of the holy-noticing lifestyle is not to avoid feelings or to detach ourselves from emotions but to notice and respond to them in a God-honoring way.**

This increased window helps decouple our brain's tendency to automatically react to stressful situations. Instead of ignoring, burying, or getting caught up in afflictive emotions, it helps us observe them dispassionately, thus deflating their power over us. It also improves resilience, the ability to bounce back from difficulty, self-awareness, how well we pick up social cues from others,[15] and positive outlook on life.[16]

Hedonic treadmill[17] is a term used to describe what some believe to be a permanent happiness set point built into us all. The theory states that we all maintain a constant level of happiness throughout our lives. Even after we experience a really good or bad event, after a time we settle back to our happiness set point. A lifestyle of holy noticing, however, can actually increase that set point, making us happier.[18]

Holy noticing also helps us deal with anxiety. Researchers have discovered three patterns that characterize and perpetuate our anxiety[19] and reveal how a mindful lifestyle helps battle those unhealthy patterns.

- *A narrow, fused, entangled focus on the feeling of anxiety.* A lifestyle of holy noticing helps anxious people broaden their awareness of their original experience. This creates a more balanced view of the original experience that created their anxiety, thus reducing their reactivity to it. This helps them make better Christ-centered decisions in the moment by focusing *on* the moment rather than a future moment potentially laden with more anxiety.

- *A desire to make the anxiety go away by suppressing it.* It helps us view our anxiety as a transient mental event (and not a fact), to accept it and ourselves better, and to judge ourselves less for feeling as we do. This can help us free our mind space to think more accurately with the mind of Christ.

- *Avoiding people and situations that might evoke anxiety.* It helps us step into life's opportunities by trusting God, even when uncertainty evokes anxiety.

Holy noticing also increases our confidence that we can more effectively weather future difficulties.[20] It develops in us the capacity to ride out our feelings in difficulty and thus avoid compulsive, unhealthy behaviors we try to use to make us feel good or avoid feeling bad.

In summary, a lifestyle of holy noticing turns down the power of our fight-flight center;[21] decreases anxiety, depression, worry, and anger; improves impulse control;[22] helps us recover faster from negative emotions;[23] and enhances happiness.[24]

Dealing with difficult emotions is like a one of those finger puzzles we won at the arcade. The puzzle (or trap) is a six-inch tube made of multicolored woven straw about the size of your index finger. You put your index finger on each hand into each end of the tube. The more you pull and struggle to remove your fingers, the tighter the trap gets. The only way to free yourself is to loosen the tension from your fingers by gently pushing *into* the tube.

In a similar way, if we struggle and fight against an afflictive emotion by trying to suppress, repress, or use the Whac-A-Mole method to make it go away, the emotion can tighten around our soul, like that trap tightens around our fingers. Trying to wrestle the emotion away habituates our desire to rid ourselves from current moments filled with unpleasant emotions that we think *must* go away for us to experience *shalom*. And when we try to push away our emotions, they end up in our bodies as headaches, shoulder tension, stomachaches, and other chronic health problems. Only when we take a Spirit-guided approach by actually leaning into the emotion, rather than forcing it away, will it lose its power. We must notice and observe it, sit with it, and describe and label it to lessen our tendency to repeatedly return to it.[25] Over time, those afflictive emotions will loosen their grip on us, and we will learn that by God's grace we no longer are at their mercy.

Most people can't accurately label their emotions. A study of more than five hundred thousand people revealed that only 36 percent could accurately identify their emotions as they occur.[26] Psychologists have coined the term *alexithymia* to explain a person's extreme inability to use words to describe their emotions. And the less we're able to describe them, the less aware we are of our internal world of thoughts and emotions.[27]

Yet it's vitally important for our emotional and spiritual health that we learn to label them and release them to the Lord. The better we can describe them, the better we can deal with the situations that caused them. And labeling our afflictive emotions actually diminishes their power.[28] As we get better at detecting them at lower intensity levels, we're more able to deal with them when they come at us with full force.

So for practice four, the *A* of the BREATHe model, you'll learn how to label and release your afflictive emotions to the Lord. Along with two visual word pictures, I give an example of what a session might look like.

Formal Practice > *A*: Label and Release Your *Afflictive* Emotions (*Affect*)

Anchor verses: Galatians 5:22–23

Skills: emotional crosshairs, quiet waters exercises

When you look into a rifle scope, you see crosshairs, which are made up of a small vertical line and a small horizontal line that intersect allowing you to pinpoint a target. In this practice, you'll learn the emotional crosshairs exercise, which can help you describe how you feel. Learning to notice, identify, and describe your emotions, both good and bad, is a crucial skill for emotional regulation.

Imagine that the vertical line represents a range of feeling from pleasant or positive at the top to unpleasant or negative at the bottom.[29] Imagine that the horizontal line represents a range of the intensity of your feelings, from fatigued or drained on the left to alert and energized on the right.[30] As you visualize the crosshairs, try to describe your feelings by placing them on both the vertical and horizontal lines. You can download the Rifle Scope Chart at www.holynoticing.com/bonus to help you if it's difficult.[31] This visual helps you evaluate your emotions on a more fluid scale rather than in a narrow way (i.e., in shades of color rather than black and white). Although a single strong emotion may seem to dominate us at times, multiple feelings and body sensations actually contribute to how we feel. The more your practice this skill, the better you will get at accurately describing how you feel.

The other skill I want to introduce is called the quiet waters exercise. In this exercise, you will picture yourself in the setting of Psalm 23. David writes,

The Lord is my shepherd, I lack nothing.
>   He makes me lie down in green pastures,
> he leads me beside quiet waters,
>   he refreshes my soul.
> He guides me along the right paths
>   for his name's sake. (1–3).

I encourage you to read the entire psalm and pay attention to these beautiful images: green pastures, quiet waters, God as a shepherd, and so on.

Now imagine you are sitting by a deep, calm river that represents God's infinite abundance of grace. Your afflictive emotions are pebbles, rocks, or even boulders that you toss into the stream and see disappear into the depths, fading out of your awareness. This is an application of Peter's instruction to: "cast all your anxiety on him because he cares for you" (1 Peter 5:7). Each time an emotion resurfaces, mentally toss it back into the water through prayer.

Now, sit in a comfortable chair, in a place free from distraction. I've written in italics what you may *think*, *verbalize*, or *pray* during the practice session, and I put in [brackets] my comments and suggestions. In this example, I will insert my breath prayers as well as other personal components as if I were doing it myself.

So, start your timer for three minutes (or twelve minutes if you are doing *B*, *R*, *E*, and *A*), get comfortable, and close your eyes to visually block any distractions. You'll probably want to read through the following section first and then practice it.

Label and Release Your
Afflictive Emotions (*Affect*)—Practice

[Begin with long, slow breaths.
Breathe in.
Breathe out.
Breathe in.
Breathe out.
Breathe in and breathe out your breath prayer.]

Holy Spirit [the in-breath]
Breathe on me [the out-breath]

[Repeat your breath prayer as long as you want. You may want to include other breath prayers, such as *Lord Jesus* (on the in-breath) and *You are good* (on the out-breath).]
[Move on to your anchor verses.]
[Meditate on them by slowly reading or reciting them from memory. If you are using Galatians 5:22–23 as your anchor verses, reflect on each quality mentioned. Visualize in your mind someone you know or yourself demonstrating love, joy, peace, and so on. Remember, you're in no rush. Take your time. And when your mind wanders, which it will, thank God for helping you recognize it. Don't berate yourself for a wandering mind. Simply refocus on your breath and pick up where you left off.]

Lord, I pause right now to be present with You and my affect, my emotions, both pleasant and afflictive ones.
I want to relate to any difficult emotions in a way that honors You and helps me release them to You.
I don't want to push them away but to acknowledge their existence even as I know Your Spirit is with me right now.
Lord, reveal to me any afflictive emotions right now.
I'm having feelings of _____.

[Label and describe how you feel, both good and bad emotions. Use the crosshairs exercise or Rifle Scope Chart if you need help. Remember, when we label our difficult emotions, their power over us decreases. Simply name and describe them without adding commentary or judgment.

Observe them without getting caught up in them or judging them as right or wrong. Remind yourself that these emotions don't define you. You aren't ascribing intent to them or evaluating them. You are simply observing them as transient passing mental events. Try to use descriptive words (i.e., *unfortunate*) rather than evaluative words (i.e., *horrible*).]

Lord, I am noticing the emotion of (anger, etc.) right now.
I acknowledge it without pushing it away.
My (anger) does not pose a threat to me. I am safe in Your care.

[Stay aware of your tendency to push away, suppress, or use the Whac-A-Mole strategy.

If you sense sin behind the emotion, confess it. But remember that a feeling does not automatically imply sin.

Once you've labeled them, it's time to release these emotions to the Lord. Turn your attention to skill 2, the quiet waters exercise from Psalm 23.]

Lord, I release my (anger, etc.) to You.
I let go of it.
May Your Spirit now grow in me greater love, joy, peace, patience,
kindness, goodness, faithfulness, gentleness, and self-control so that
I don't try to suppress my emotions or let them control me.
Thank You, Lord, for helping me.

[end of the practice]

You can probably read through the above practice in sixty seconds. However, your goal is not to rush through but to calm your heart and simply be with your afflictive emotions, observe them, label them, and release them to the Lord. Again, a negative emotion does not necessarily imply sin. What we do with our emotions leads us to sin. As you practice being with your afflictive emotions more often, you will actually reconfigure and strengthen healthy brain connections aligned with positive emotions[32] that will help you more consistently deal with the negative ones.[33]

In the next chapter we'll look at holy noticing as it relates to our thoughts. You'll probably notice some overlap between this practice and the next because we don't naturally separate a thought from an emotion. They are seamlessly woven together like a soundtrack in a movie. When absorbed in a great movie, we seldom separate the music from the dialogue. It's all one experience for us. Our thoughts and emotions work together much like that.

Chapter Summary

- **Practice Four in the BREATHe Model:** "*A*: Label and Release Your *Afflictive* Emotions (*Affect*)." You learned how holy noticing can help you label and release your afflictive emotions to the Lord.

- **Anchor Verses:** Galatians 5:22–23

- **Visual Metaphors**: crosshairs in a rifle scope; quiet waters

- **Skills:** emotional crosshairs, quiet waters exercises (labeling your emotions, releasing your afflictive emotions to the Lord)

• **Practice Steps:**

1) *Formal practice*: During each of the next five days,
   take twelve minutes to try all four practices—"*B*:
   Ponder and Yield Your *Body*" (use the body scan,
   gratefulness exercises); "*R:* Review and Renew Your
   Relationships" (use the concentric circles exercise);
   "*E:* Notice and Engage Your *Environment*" (use
   the deep listening, focused observation exercises);
   and "*A:* Label and Release Your *Afflictive* Emotions
   (*Affect*)" (use the emotional crosshairs, quiet waters
   exercises).

2) *"e: Engage the World like Christ" practice*: Try to
   check in to your emotional state several times each
   day. When you sense a difficult emotion rising,
   practice the *A* exercise. When you sense a positive
   emotion, pause, feel it deeply, and thank the Lord
   for it. Finally, when you feel difficult emotions, ask
   yourself if your behavior toward others is being
   negatively affected. If it is, ask the Lord to empower
   you to act in ways that honor Him, even though you
   may not feel like acting in those ways.

Bonus material available at www.holynoticing.com/bonus:

• The RAIN tool for dealing with afflictive emotions

• Emotional Processing Style Tool

• Rifle Scope Chart to help you describe your emotions.

CHAPTER 8

Practice Five: Observe and Submit Your Thoughts

Keep your mind strictly in the presence of God.
—BROTHER LAWRENCE

*Someone once said that the deepest problem in prayer
is often not the absence of God but the absence of me.
I'm not actually there. My mind is everywhere.*
—ROWAN WILLIAMS, FORMER ARCHBISHOP OF CANTERBURY

CHAPTER BIG IDEA: This chapter unpacks the *T* in the BREATHe model. *T* stands for "Observe and Submit Your *Thoughts*." In this chapter you'll learn a skill to make you more readily aware of your thoughts, especially those that are erroneous, unhealthy, or even sinful, and more prone to think true and wholesome thoughts.

ONE MORNING DURING MY DEVOTIONAL time, I was on *E* in the BREATHe model when I looked out the window at the forest behind our home. As I praised God for His creativity and the warm spring day, my thoughts unconsciously floated to fall and football. I grew up in the southern US, and each fall I look forward to college and NFL football. The prior year my favorite NFL team, the Atlanta Falcons, had squandered a huge lead in the Super Bowl, and lost. That was a bad day for me.

As I sat in my rocker that morning, however, I began

imagining myself in church the next Sunday, sheepishly asking the congregation to pray for me so that I would never get caught up in NFL football like that again. Then I realized, *What? I'm supposed to be praying and practicing holy noticing. Why am I thinking about football?*

My mind had drifted from celebrating God's creative work in nature to football to fall to the Falcons to church. Mind wandering is common even when we spend time with God, because that's how our brains work. Our attention easily drifts from the present moment to just about anything. Oswald Chambers wrote, "The most difficult thing to do is to pray. We cannot seem to get our minds into good working order, and the first thing we have to fight is wandering thoughts. The great battle in private prayer is overcoming this problem of our idle and wandering thinking."[1]

When we practice holy noticing, we battle not only mind wandering but also narrow and unbiblical thinking as well. Professor Martin Laird paints a profound picture of the plight of our minds and hearts when he tells a story about an unusual sight he saw during one of his daily walks. His route led him across open fields where he frequently noticed a man walking his three Kerry blue terriers. Two of the dogs exuded energy, speed, and grace as they bounded through the fields. But although the third dog would run, it ran in tight little circles.

One day Dr. Laird mustered the courage to ask the owner why this dog ran in such a strange way. The man explained that before he acquired him, the dog "had lived practically all its life in a cage and could only exercise by running in circles. For this dog, to run meant to run in tight circles. So instead of bounding through the open fields that surrounded it, it ran in circles."[2]

Sometimes our minds can keep us in similar mental cages, our thoughts running in repetitive mental loops, like a DVD that gets stuck repeating a scene.

Rather than running in open fields of God's grace, we run in small, tight mental circles.

Rather than running in open fields of God's grace, we run in small, tight mental circles.

Our minds act like an inner narrator that has something to say about everything, imbuing judgments and evaluations with emotion, and then projecting these thoughts on the screen of our minds. Like an incessant chatterbox, this inner narrator is often biased and confused. As we become embroiled in our thoughts, we pay undue attention to them and create stories about life that often don't reflect reality. We become players in an unhealthy drama playing out in our minds.

Also, since our brains are designed to run as efficiently as possible, to conserve energy we take subconscious mental shortcuts called heuristics. Heuristics aren't all bad because if we consciously thought through every potential decision, our brains would fry. Problems arise, though, when we take those shortcuts based on wrong information.

We too easily assume our thoughts are true without questioning them. As they merge with our emotions, they produce turbocharged responses[3] and become extremely vivid, like the color in ultra HD televisions. Thoughts and feelings intertwine because our fight-flight center reaches into our brain stem to trigger our brain's emotional accelerator and also into our brain's CEO to change our thinking. So emotions can cause thoughts and thoughts can cause emotions.[4]

We become riveted to the "looping DVD" in our minds

because thoughts course through our brains between 12,000 and 60,000 times each day, even though scientists differ on the exact number.[5] Even though they're made of tiny doses of chemicals and miniscule amounts of electricity, thoughts wield disproportionate power over our lives compared to their biochemical strength. We soon identify with and believe those thoughts. Like a mental whisk, we stir up our emotions and thoughts into a frothy mess, hindering us from being present in the moment for others and for God. It's like having hundreds of cable-TV channels in your mind but getting stuck on the anxiety or worry channel.

If we don't check our thoughts, they can become our identity, because we rehearse and ruminate over them in an ongoing inner commentary. Then, networks of neurons are created in our brains around those unhealthy thought patterns. We begin to believe we are ugly, fat, unlovable, stupid, or that nobody cares for us, including God.

This process is similar to how a stream becomes a creek, which can eventually grow into a river. As water continues to flow in the same course over time, the channel is deepened and the river's border widened. Yet you can change a river's direction the same way it was formed. You begin to divert that water a bit at a time in a different direction. Slowly it becomes a new stream, then a creek, and then a river.

Our brains work in the same way. We can change unhealthy thinking patterns by creating new neural pathways, just like a river can be diverted by creating a new channel. Holy noticing helps us do that by creating new mental pathways that are aligned with truth, rather than with lies and distortions. This helps the parts of our brain that encourage the endless DVD loop to function more accurately.[6]

How Holy Noticing Benefits Our Thinking

Holy noticing brings two fundamental benefits to our thinking: (1) we can see our thoughts more clearly, and (2) we can avoid thinking traps.

Holy noticing helps us see our thoughts more clearly.

When difficult or painful thoughts arise, we often try to avoid, analyze, fix, or judge them as if our thoughts were facts. Holy noticing, however, helps us first step back to simply *be* with the thoughts, and with the discomfort they may bring. This makes space for the Holy Spirit to do His work of healing, however He sees fit. Instead of trying to get rid of the thought or solve it, we allow it to come to the surface and submit it to the Lord.

The desert monastics called this process *apatheia*, which can be translated as "mindful attention."[7] Through their spiritual practice, they learned not only to become aware of their thoughts and desires but also to be with them without feeling "compelled to fulfil them."[8]

Our busy, agitated, and distracted minds are like a glass filled with muddy water. As long as it is agitated, the mud clouds the water and doesn't allow light to pass through. However, if the glass remains still, after a few minutes the mud will settle so that the water becomes clear. Holy noticing helps settle our thoughts and emotions so that we can see our inner world more clearly, observing our thoughts more like objects. Second Corinthians 10:5 describes it this way: "We demolish arguments and every pretension that sets itself up against the knowledge of God, and we take captive every thought to make it obedient to Christ."

In this verse, Paul uses a military metaphor to parallel our thoughts and philosophies to actual things—in this case enemy combatants captured in war. He describes thoughts as objects to be reckoned with, or taken captive, rather than ethereal objects. Holy noticing helps us look *at* our thoughts as a detached observer, rather than experiencing life *from* our unfiltered and often incorrect thoughts.[9] Thus we avoid both overly identifying with them and getting caught up in our inner commentary about them.[10]

Holy noticing can help us disconnect from our thoughts so that we can clearly see them for what they are—discrete mental events—and avoid misidentifying with them. It's like being able to remove the proverbial rose-colored glasses from our eyes and realizing that our thoughts and emotions have colored our world. We are then able to describe our thoughts and emotions rather than be defined by them.

Another helpful metaphor involves imagining you are standing on a bridge watching three trains go by below. One author describes it this way:

> As you look down, imagine that the train to the left carries only the "ore" of things you notice in the present moment. That ore is composed of sensations, perceptions, and emotions. It carries things like the sounds you hear; sweaty palms you feel; skipped heartbeats you sense; sadness you notice; and so forth. The middle train carries only your thoughts: your evaluations, your predictions, your self-conceptualizations, and so on. The train on your right carries your urges to act; your pull to avoid and look away; and your efforts to change the subject. Looking down on these three tracks can be seen as a metaphor for looking at your mind.[11]

Holy noticing helps us stay on the "bridge" to notice our thoughts, without giving in to faulty thinking or sinful behavior. And it makes us aware if we've hopped into one of the trains so that we can go back to the bridge. It helps us learn to see our thoughts as not necessarily reflecting reality or truth. Rather, we see them as what they are, mental events rather than objective facts. For example, if we berate ourselves about something and tell ourselves that we were foolish, that thought may or may not be true. And even if the behavior was foolish, it does not mean that we are by nature foolish. The thought is often simply an event in our mind. The goal is to look *at* our thoughts and emotions rather than *from* them.[12]

Holy noticing helps us avoid common thinking traps.

God has given our minds an incredible ability to think about the past and imagine the future. Scripture tells us to reflect on God's deeds in the past and anticipate Jesus' return in the future (see Matt. 24:42, Ps. 77:11). Unfortunately, as a result of the fall, these mental abilities often don't work well. We obsess about what's wrong in the present. We anticipate the future, and worry about it, projecting worst-case scenarios into it. We think about the past, and regret and ruminate over it. And we extrapolate past pain into the future. Fearful foreboding, anticipation,

> **Scripture tells us to reflect on God's deeds in the past (Ps. 77:11) and anticipate Jesus' return in the future (Matt. 24:42).**

and conjecture make potential future events larger than they ever will be. Chronic stress can cause us to easily fall into these unhealthy thinking traps.

Read the list of thinking traps below and assess yourself by answering either *seldom, sometimes,* or *often.*

THINKING TRAPS ASSESSMENT										
Thinking Trap	Seldom				Sometimes					Often
1. I imagine worst-case scenarios (catastrophizing).	1	2	3	4	5	6	7	8	9	10
2. I exaggerate the negative or discount the positive.	1	2	3	4	5	6	7	8	9	10
3. I convince myself that I know what people are thinking (mind reading).	1	2	3	4	5	6	7	8	9	10
4. I live by a list of unbreakable rules for myself or others.	1	2	3	4	5	6	7	8	9	10
5. I hold others responsible for my pain or hold myself responsible for others' pain (blame).[13]	1	2	3	4	5	6	7	8	9	10
6. I assume things are true because they "feel" true.	1	2	3	4	5	6	7	8	9	10
7. I see things as either black or white with little in between (black-and-white thinking).	1	2	3	4	5	6	7	8	9	10
8. I am hypervigilant about some things (tunnel vision).	1	2	3	4	5	6	7	8	9	10
9. When something goes wrong, I attribute it to something I did (personalizing).	1	2	3	4	5	6	7	8	9	10
10. When I try to make a decision, I get stuck by doubting myself (overthinking).[14]	1	2	3	4	5	6	7	8	9	10

How did you do? If you scored high on some of these, holy noticing will be a spiritual discipline that can help you recognize those traps you've fallen into and then help you avoid them. Dr. Curt Thompson notes that it will "enable us to pay attention to our minds in order to pay attention to the Spirit who is speaking to us through that very medium."[15]

It will help you detach from wrong thinking in the same way that food detaches from Teflon. When you cook something in a Teflon-coated pan, food simply slides off because it doesn't stick. When you detach from these thoughts, you don't overly identify with them by getting hooked on your evaluations and judgments of them. You realize you are not those thoughts. Rather, you are a person who is aware of those thoughts. You are stepping back to gain a wide-angle perspective of the situation and the thoughts that resulted. John wrote about this in 1 John 2:15–16 when he admonished us to not love the world (become overly attached to it).

Other mental benefits of holy noticing include improved working memory,[16] reducing mental fatigue,[17] increasing mental flexibility,[18] and even enhanced creativity and insight.[19]

The Weather of Our Thoughts

Mountains play a role in the lives of several prominent biblical characters: Moses received the law on Mount Sinai, Elijah heard God's gentle voice while on Mount Horeb, and David often wrote about Mount Zion in the Psalms. One of David's most famous references to Moun Zion is in Psalm 125:1: "Those who trust in the LORD are like Mount Zion, which cannot be shaken but endures forever." Here Mount Zion symbolizes God's power, blessing, and protection.

When we trust the Lord by redirecting our thinking, we are like a mountain responding to weather. Mountains are surrounded by various weather conditions—sunshine, clouds, fog, rain, thunder and lightning, blizzards. Even so, the mountain does not become the weather. In a sense, it simply observes it. In Christ, we are like that mountain with all kinds of external and internal weather around us, made up of our circumstances, emotions, and thoughts. We may prefer certain kinds of weather, but we are not the weather. Some of those negative internal weather events are not really us (fear, worry, anxiety). Some may reflect sinful attitudes in our hearts that require confession. Others definitely reflect what Christ gives us (love, joy, peace).

In other words, your anxious and afflictive thoughts and emotions are, in sum, not you. They do not reflect your identity in Christ. They are your emotional and mental weather. Holy noticing helps us keep this perspective. The mountain metaphor applies specifically to our thought life. Paul writes in Philippians 4:8, "Finally, brothers, whatever is true, whatever is noble, whatever is right, whatever is pure, whatever is lovely, whatever is admirable—if anything is excellent or praiseworthy—think about such things." When we redirect our thoughts from the endless loops playing in our minds to thinking about the qualities Paul mentioned, we remind ourselves that in Christ we are that mountain and not the weather.[20] We're applying what Peter advised when he said his letters were intended to "stimulate you to wholesome thinking" (2 Peter 3:1).

Christian neuroscientist Jeffrey Schwartz coined the phrase "survival of the busiest"[21] (the thoughts we most think about stick the most in our minds), which reflects the apostle Paul's insights. In other words, the more we think certain thoughts, both healthy and unhealthy, the more powerful those thoughts become. The most active thoughts survive.

If we don't pay attention to our thinking, we become captive to the changing weather patterns of our lives—our emotions, moods, thoughts, experiences, anything and every-thing of which we have little awareness. These thoughts can blind and victimize us. We can let them become us or convince ourselves that they are us, when in reality they are just the weather in our minds.

So, paying attention to our thoughts and emotions without becoming overly attached to them is key to spiritual and emo-tional well-being and *shalom*. Holy noticing gives us a different vantage point from which to observe our thoughts. As we wit-ness them, it takes us off the "hair trigger that compels us to react to things as soon as they happen."[22] Paul didn't know brain science, but the author of brain science, God Himself, gave him insight about our minds long before science caught up.

This perspective does not mean we never judge our thoughts. A hateful, vengeful, or lustful thought must be confessed as sin. And sometimes Satan tempts us with evil thoughts, or some experience stirs a temptation to think an evil thought. Rather than immediately dismissing such thoughts as *not* sinful or quickly labeling them *as* sinful, holy noticing helps us give appropriate attention to them so that the Holy Spirit can bring conviction should we need to confess the thought as sin.

Along with a word picture (weather on a mountain), be-low I give an example of what a session might look it—the thoughts, prayers, and activities in it.

Formal Practice > *T*: Observe and Submit Your *Thoughts*
Anchor verses: 2 Corinthians 10:5;
Romans 12:2; Philippians 4:8; Isaiah 26:3

Skills: thinking about your thinking or reflec-
tive thinking
(metacognition) exercise

When you begin this practice, it might be a bit
challenging because we often don't want to be left
alone with our thoughts. In studies at Harvard University, college-aged
participants were asked to sit in a room and "entertain themselves with
their thoughts." They were allowed to think about anything. Before they
entered the research room, they had to leave behind anything that could
distract them, such as books, cell phones, and writing materials. In one
part of the experiment, the researchers attached an electrode to each
of the subjects' ankles, allowing the students to self-administer a mild
electrical shock. Several opted to shock themselves, just to do something
rather than be with their thoughts.[23] The researchers concluded that
many people would rather do something, even if it's potentially harmful,
than simply be with their thoughts.

If this practice becomes uncomfortable, remember that it may take
time to learn to be with your thoughts. As you take small steps forward
by incorporating this practice into your devotional time, being with your
thoughts will become easier. As you begin, remember that only the Lord
knows all your thoughts and that He knows them better than you do (Jer.
17:9–10; Prov. 21:2). And to avoid unhealthy introspection, heed the
advice of Scottish pastor Robert Murray McCheyne: "For every look at
yourself, take ten looks at Christ."[24]

Sit in a comfortable chair, in a place free from distraction. I've written in *italics* what you may *think*, *verbalize*, or *pray* during the practice

session, and I put in [brackets] my comments and suggestions. In this example I will insert my breath prayers as well as other personal components as if I were doing it myself. I suggest you read through the exercise first.

Now you are ready. Get comfortable, start your timer for three minutes (or fifteen minutes if you are combining *B, R, E, A,* and *T*), and close your eyes to visually block distractions.

Observe and Submit Your *Thoughts*—Practice

[Begin with long, slow breaths.
Breathe in.
Breathe out.
Breathe in.
Breathe out.
Breathe in and breathe out with your breath prayer.]

Holy Spirit [the in-breath]
Breathe on me [the out-breath]

[Repeat your breath prayer as long as you want. You may want to include other breath prayers such as *Lord Jesus* (on the in-breath) *You are good* (on the out-breath).]
[Move on to your anchor verses. Meditate on them by reading or reciting them from memory.]

Lord, I submit my thoughts to You right now.
Help me sort through which thoughts are true and correct and
which are not.
Help me be with my thoughts without adding commentary to them.

[As thoughts rise up in your mind, try to reframe troublesome ones such as *I am anxious* to a decentered thought such as *I am having feelings of anxiety*, which provokes less anxiety. By labeling thoughts in this way, you're adding some distance between them and their effects on you. Other phrases could include, *I am having memories of . . . , feelings that . . . , thoughts about . . . , bodily sensations of . . .* , and so on.

Try to simply name your thought instead of spinning a commentary about it. Remember, you are developing the skill of thinking about your thinking (metacognition), the ability to think about your own mental state. As you grow in a holy-noticing lifestyle, you'll get better at this.[25]

One helpful way to distance yourself from your unhealthy thoughts is to learn to differentiate between a description and an evaluation. A description is just that, a description of an event or an emotion. An evaluation attributes subjective qualities to an event. For example, a description would be: "I am having feelings of fear." An evaluation would be: "My fear is intolerable." Evaluations often intensify our emotions.

Imagine that you are on a mountain and are observing the weather. You are secure in the Lord, and your difficult thoughts are like the weather. [View those thoughts as passing storms.]

Lord, I submit this thought to You: [fill in the blank]
And this one . . .
And this one . . .
Help me be present with these thoughts.
Thank You that I am not my thoughts.
I am as secure as Mount Zion. You are my rock, my fortress, my strength, my truth.

[Here you may want to recall and reflect on your anchor verses again. There is no need to try to dredge up negative thoughts. As thoughts arise, even good ones, be present with them. If thoughts arise that are potentially sinful, bring those before the Holy Spirit and let Him bring appropriate conviction. Confess those that He convicts you are sinful.]

Lord, help me live out the reality of having the mind of Christ.
I want to think thoughts that honor You.
I submit my thinking to You.

[end of the practice]

So by now you've tried the first five practices: *B, R, E, A,* and *T.* Try to to do all five together, one after the other. The more you practice, the easier it becomes. You don't need to repeat your breath prayers between each practice, unless your mind wanders. When it does, take a few slow breaths and then spell the acronym BREATHe to get you back to the practice you left when your mind wandered.

We've almost covered every practice in the BREATHe model. In the next chapter we'll look at the final piece, *H*: Search and Surrender your *Heart.*

Chapter Summary

- **Practice Five in the BREATHe Model:** "*T*: Observe and Submit Your *Thoughts*." You learned how holy noticing can make you more readily aware of your thoughts, especially those that are erroneous, unhealthy, or even sinful, and more prone to think true and wholesome thoughts.

- **Anchor Verses:** 2 Corinthians 10:5; Romans 12:2; Philippians 4:8; Isaiah 26:3

- **Visual Metaphor:** weather on a mountain

- **Skills:** thinking about your thinking or reflective thinking (metacognition) exercise

- **Practice Steps**:

  1) *Formal practice*: During each of the next five days, add this practice to the first four practices and take about fifteen minutes to practice all five—"*B*: Ponder and Yield Your *Body*" (use the body scan, gratefulness exercises); "*R*: Review and Renew Your *Relationships*" (use the concentric circles exercise); "*E*: Notice and Engage Your *Environment*" (use the deep listening, focused observation exercises); "*A*: Label and Release Your *Afflictive* Emotions (*Affect*)" (use the emotional crosshairs, quiet waters exercises); and "*T*: Observe and Submit Your *Thoughts*" (use the thinking about your thinking exercise).

  2) *"e: Engage the World like Christ" practice*: Just as you checked in with your emotions in the prior chapter's practice steps, do the same for your thoughts. Periodically ask yourself what you are thinking at the moment. If you're dwelling on negative and unwholesome thoughts, recite Philippians 4:8 to reorient your thinking.

Bonus material available at www.holynoticing.com/bonus:

- How We Change chart
- The 5-R's when Your Mind Wanders

CHAPTER 9

Practice Six: Search and Surrender Your Heart

Let us . . . [fix] our eyes on Jesus.
—HEBREWS 12:1–2

*The neurological activity between our ears . . .
has a direct link to our formation into Christlikeness.*
—TRICIA McCARY RHODES

CHAPTER BIG IDEA: This chapter unpacks the *H* in the BREATHe model. *H* stands for "Search and Surrender Your *Heart*." In this chapter, you'll learn how holy noticing helps us grow our faith, grow in character, and discern the Spirit's promptings.

WHAT BEGAN AS A NORMAL DAY in seminary became one remembered with great chagrin for decades to come.[1]

In 1973, forty seminary students volunteered for a study at Princeton University. The instructors, who were the researchers in this experiment, explained to each student that their assignment was about religious education and vocation. Each participant would first complete a questionnaire and then walk to another building for further instructions. Once there, each participant received their assignment. Some were asked to prepare a talk on seminary jobs, while others were asked to prepare a talk on the parable of the Good Samaritan. Each participant was then instructed to go to another building to give their talk. Some were told to hurry to avoid being late.

Unbeknownst to the participants, however, the researchers had placed an actor, who was part of the experiment, in a courtyard that each student had to pass through on their way to the other building. He was slumped over and moaning in pain, obviously needing help.

What factor made the biggest difference in whether or not a student stopped to help? The result surprised the researchers.

The subject of their talk did not influence whether or not a student stopped to help the person in need. Even those who prepared the talk on the Good Samaritan were no more likely to stop and help than the ones who prepared a talk on seminary jobs. The common factor? Hurry.

Those who were in less of a rush stopped more often than those who had been told to hurry. Hurry influenced the frequency with which the students noticed the person in need. Hurry had marginalized their values in the moment.

> Holy noticing trains us to be more present in each moment and more mindful of Jesus and the needs of others. It develops our ability to fix our eyes on Him moment-by-moment (Heb. 12:1–2).

This experiment reminds us that when we rush through life to get the next better moment, we often fail to notice God's prompting to act with Christ-centered compassion toward others. Holy noticing, however, trains us to be more present in each moment and more mindful of Jesus and the needs of others. It develops our ability to fix our eyes on Him moment-by-moment (Heb. 12:1–2).

How Holy Noticing
Benefits Your Heart and Soul

The book of Proverbs emphasizes the important role of your heart when it notes,

Above all else, guard your heart,
    for everything you do flows from it.
Keep your mouth free of perversity;
    keep corrupt talk far from your lips.
Let your eyes look straight ahead;
    fix your gaze directly before you.
Give careful thought to the paths for your feet
    and be steadfast in all your ways. (4:23–26)

Your heart shapes your actions. In Scripture, the heart refers to more than just our emotions or reasoning ability. Rather, it plays a more comprehensive role because from it everything else flows—your deepest loves, trusts, and commitments. Tim Keller writes, "What the heart most loves and trusts, the mind finds reasonable, the emotions find desirable, and the will finds doable."[2] Research indicates that holy noticing builds the following heart qualities.[3]

> Your heart shapes your actions. It plays a more comprehensive role because from it everything else flows—your deepest loves, trusts, and commitments.

Holy noticing helps us resist temptation.

Scripture reminds us that God will give us what we need to

resist temptation: "No temptation has seized you except what is common to mankind. And God is faithful; he will not let you be tempted beyond what you can bear. But when you are tempted, he will also provide a way out so that you can endure it" (1 Cor. 10:13). But how do we put that into practice? By applying the skills you're learning about holy noticing.

In one study of smokers, paying attention to their temptation to smoke actually decreased the frequency they later smoked because it decreased their cravings.[4] Holy noticing bolsters internal strength to resist mindless impulses.[5] And in general a mindful lifestyle strengthens moral and ethical decision-making.[6]

Holy noticing helps form us spiritually.

Someone once asked Jesus to name the greatest commandment. He responded by saying we are to love God with our whole being. He then said the second greatest commandment was to love our neighbor as ourselves (Luke 10:27). Holy noticing enables us to live out both of these commandments through the work of the Holy Spirit.

The Holy Spirit conforms us to Jesus' likeness through a process called sanctification (Rom. 8:29; Eph. 4:13; Gal. 4:19). As He changes our beliefs, our conduct and character also change. The early desert fathers and mothers applied this truth because for them, "mindfulness of God became the new compass direction for inner transformation."[7]

Christian philosopher J. P. Moreland writes that the three traits determining how a core belief impacts our behavior are its content, strength, and centrality.[8] *Content* refers to what we believe about it. *Strength* refers to how convinced we are that it is true. *Centrality* relates to how important the belief is relative to all other beliefs. For example, if I believe sweet potatoes are good for me, the strength of my belief may or may not lead me to eat them. However, if that belief is central to my other beliefs about diet, I will more likely eat them. (For the record, I do not like sweet potatoes!)

Spiritual formation, another term for discipleship or spiritual growth, involves changing our core beliefs. Moreland explains

> **The more we reflect on, mull over, and meditate on Scripture and the nature of God and His work, the more we sculpt our brain pathways toward a lifestyle that more consistently reflects Christlike behavior and belief.**

that although we can't directly change those beliefs by an exercise of our will, we can "change them indirectly through . . . engaging in activities of the mind such as study, meditation, and reflection that would change the content, strength, and centrality of our belief(s)."[9] That's how holy noticing changes our character.[10] The more we reflect on, mull over, and meditate on Scripture and the nature of God and His work, the more we sculpt the pathways in our brains toward a lifestyle that more consistently reflects Christlike behavior and belief.

Spiritual transformation through Christ involves the whole brain. The CEO in our brains helps us understand and apply biblical truth. Our emotional centers add a feeling component, a sense of warmth toward and longing for God. Our memory centers help us recall Scripture and God's acts of faithfulness. Other parts of our brains motivate us to tangible action. The Holy Spirit involves all these parts to make us more like Jesus.[11] Holy noticing strengthens the parts of our brains related to character and gives us greater control over the fear, anxiety, and anger areas of our brains that often hinder spiritual transformation.[12]

Holy noticing helps us have a healthy view of ourselves.

As an expansion on the above benefit, holy noticing helps us develop a healthy view of ourselves, sometimes called self-compassion. This perspective isn't self-centeredness or self-preoccupation. Rather, it's refusing to base our inherent value and self-worth on approval from others or on our performance. This is a healthy mindset devoid of self-loathing.

Augustine wrote in *City of God* (10:3), "First see whether you have learned to love yourself. . . . If you have not learned how to love yourself, I am afraid that you will cheat your neighbor as yourself." If we don't legitimately care for and respect ourselves, we cannot love God or others as we should. Jesus Himself modeled self-care when He withdrew from the crowds to replenish His soul and commune with His heavenly Father (Mark 1:35; Luke 5:16; Matt. 14:23).

When we learn to love ourselves appropriately through holy noticing, we quiet the centers of our brains that produce negative emotions,[13] become less prone to people please,[14] become less self-critical,[15] and enhance our overall mental health.[16]

Holy noticing makes us more sensitive to the Holy Spirit.

Your conscious mind is like a boardroom table where the leaders of different departments come together to make decisions. These leaders tend to operate independently. Yet, if the company as a whole expects to accomplish anything worthwhile, these leaders must gather to discuss and analyze issues so they can align their efforts. This is a helpful metaphor for the many streams of information that come into our minds and brains.

Those streams of information include our physical senses—taste, touch, hearing, smell, and sight. However, other neuro-biological senses "sit at the table" as well, such as our ability to think about our thinking,[17] sensing our inner body states like hunger and disgust,[18] intuiting the feelings and intentions of others,[19] and knowing where our body is in space.[20]

As in any company boardroom, someone must lead the discussion or else chaos ensues. Imagine that the most important person sitting at the table is the Holy Spirit. He *should* play the prominent role in a believer's decision-making, attitudes, and behavior, surpassing the influence of the others at the table.

Unfortunately, the others at the table are often louder, so they crowd out His gentle, quiet voice. Some voices simply take over: the ruminating thoughts that get stuck on some regret from the past, the worried fixating on a potential problem in the future, depressive emotions that color everything else, and so on. Each voice competes to be heard. Yet the Holy Spirit waits for a surrendered heart and a quieted soul, which a lifestyle of holy noticing can foster.

> **The Holy Spirit waits for a surrendered heart and a quieted soul, which a lifestyle of holy noticing can foster.**

Oswald Chambers captures this idea with these words:

> The voice of the Spirit of God is as gentle as a summer breeze—so gentle that unless you are living in complete fellowship and oneness with God, you will never hear it. The sense of warning and restraint that the Spirit gives

comes to us in the most amazingly gentle ways. And if you are not sensitive enough to detect His voice, you will quench it, and your spiritual life will be impaired. This sense of restraint will always come as a "still small voice" (1 Kings 19:12), so faint that no one except a saint of God will notice it.[21]

So how does holy noticing come into play at this "boardroom" table? It helps us make sense of, create space for, and wisely discern the weight we give to the other streams of information. It elevates the quiet voice of the Spirit by dampening the trifecta voices of fear, anxiety, and worry. It quiets mental static and neural noise.[22] It helps us filter out unbiblical thoughts and afflictive emotions, or at least give them less time at the table.

It also helps us constructively leverage these other voices (which can offer positive input) and heightens our ability to pay better attention to what truly needs our attention. And though we live between the *now* and the *not yet* of God's kingdom, holy noticing helps quiet our souls in the midst of the frenetic noise that often drowns out the Spirit's gentle whispers.

Holy noticing develops empathy and compassion to help alleviate another's suffering.

Paul commands us to "in humility value others above yourselves, not looking to your own interests but each of you to the interests of others" (Phil. 2:3–4). Unfortunately, compassion toward others in our culture has markedly decreased over the last few years.[23]

Holy noticing affects three brain processes that foster empathy and our desire to help others. It decreases the activity of the brain's fight-flight center, the amygdala, thus relieving personal distress. Second, it increases activation in parts of the brain related to goal-directed behavior, where decision-making would occur to help another. Finally, it connects our brain's CEO, pleasure center, and insula together (where the brain registers internal body sensations). As these three processes occur, it increases our disposition to help others.[24] We become more empathetic and compassionate.[25]

In one interesting study[26] some participants completed a mindfulness course, while others did not. After the study ended, the participants were invited back to the lab for further research. Unbeknownst to them, a situation was manufactured to see who would give up their chair in the waiting room to a woman who came in on crutches and was clearly in pain. She was a part of the study, but the participants didn't know that. Only 16 percent of the control group (given no mindfulness training) gave up their seats, while 37 percent of the those who had received training gave up theirs.

God designed our brains to experience pleasure when we show empathy and serve others. When we cultivate loving concern toward others, our brain's circuit for happiness energizes and "boosts the connections between the brain's circuits for joy and happiness and the prefrontal cortex, a zone critical for guiding behavior."[27] And one expert explains that the trust hormone, oxytocin, "generates the empathy that drives moral behavior, which inspires trust, which causes the release of more oxytocin, which creates more empathy."[28] Of course for a Christian, Jesus is our ultimate driver of moral behavior as we yield to the renewing work of His Spirit (see Titus 3:5). Science simply illustrates how holy-noticing practices can encourage spiritual growth. The apostle Paul wrote of his joy that God who has begun a good work in us will "carry it on to completion until the day of Christ Jesus" (Phil. 1:6).

Other benefits include a greater willingness to forgive,[29] an increase in resilience enabling us to bounce back from difficulty or failure,[30] more personal peace,[31] and less racial bias.[32]

So for the *H* of the BREATHe model, you'll learn how to search and surrender your heart to the Lord. Along with a visual word picture, I give an example of what a session might look it—the thoughts, prayers, and activities in it.

Formal Practice > *H*: Search and Surrender Your *Heart*
Anchor verses: Psalm 139:23–24; Zepheniah 3:17

Skills: openheartedness, spiritual vulnerability exercise

In this practice you'll simply open your heart to be vulnerable to what the Lord reveals. I envision the Holy Spirit shining a spotlight on my heart to reveal any sin (Ps. 139:23–24) and to shine into my heart His love, mercy, and grace. Don't make this practice only about confession of sin, although that's part of it. Make a point of receiving God's loving affirmation as expressed by the prophet Zephaniah in one of today's anchor verses I suggest:

> "For the Lord your God is living among you.
>> He is a mighty savior.
> He will take delight in you with gladness.
>> With his love, he will calm all your fears.
>> He will rejoice over you with joyful songs."
> (Zeph. 3:17 NLT)

As you practice searching and surrendering your heart, revel in this truth.

Recall once again our definition of holy noticing: *noticing, with a holy purpose, God and His handiwork, our relationships, and our inner world of thoughts and feelings.*

Now sit in a comfortable chair, in a place free from distraction. I've written in italics what you may *think, verbalize,* or *pray* during the practice session, and I put in [brackets] my comments and suggestions. In this example, I will insert my breath prayers as well as other personal components as if I were doing it myself.

So, start your timer for three minutes (or eighteen minutes if you are doing *B, R, E, A, T,* and *H*), get comfortable, and close your eyes to visually block any distractions. You'll probably want to read through the following section first and then practice it.

Search and Surrender Your *Heart*—Practice

[Begin with long, slow breaths.
Breathe in.
Breathe out.
Breathe in.
Breathe out.
Breathe in and breathe out with your breath prayer.]

Holy Spirit [the in-breath]
Breathe on me [the out-breath]

[Repeat your breath prayer as long as you want. You may want to include other breath prayers such as *Lord Jesus* (on the in-breath) *You are good* (on the out-breath).]

[Move on to your anchor verses. Meditate on them by reading or reciting them from memory.]

Lord, I yield my heart to You right now.
Please shine Your searchlight on my soul.

[Envision a bright searchlight shining on your heart.]

Reveal to me any hidden sin or wrong attitudes.

[Pause and simply be still before the Lord.
As God reveals sin, respond with confession.
After a few moments, reflect on Zephaniah 3:17 or Scriptures that clarify
your position and identity in Christ.]

Lord, I rejoice in the fact that You rejoice and sing over me.
I receive Your affirmations of my identity and position in Christ.

[One way to experience this is to recall times when you felt truly loved
by others. Recall the details of those experiences. You may want to write
them down.

You may want to list your strengths and thank God for them.
Beware of any tendency to criticize yourself or bring up your flaws.
Remember, God takes great delight in you and rejoices over you.
He loves you with an everlasting love.]

Lord, thank You for Your love, mercy, care, and concern for me.
I receive it with gratefulness.

[end of the practice]

So by now you've tried all six specifc practices, *B, R, E, A, T,
H,* plus the *e.* Try to do all six together, one after the other, once
each day during the next five days. I've included an entire session

of all the practices in appendix A. The more you practice, the easier it becomes. You don't need to repeat your breath prayers between each practice, unless your mind wanders. When it does, take a few slow breaths and then spell the acronym BREATHe to get you back to the practice you left when your mind wandered.

Chapter Summary

- **Practice Six in the BREATHe Model:** "*H*: Search and Surrender Your *Heart*." You learned how holy noticing can help you grow your faith, grow in character, and discern the Spirit's promptings.

- **Anchor Verses:** Psalm 139:23–24; Zephaniah 3:17

- **Visual Metaphor:** spotlight

- **Skills:** openheartedness, spiritual vulnerability exercise

- **Practice Steps:**

  1) *Formal practice*: During each of the next five days, add this practice to the first five practices and take about twenty minutes to practice all six at once— "*B*: Ponder and Yield Your *Body*" (use the body scan, gratefulness exercises); "*R*: Review and Renew Your *Relationships*" (use the concentric circles exercise); "*E*: Notice and Engage Your *Environment*" (use the deep listening, focused observation exercise); "*A*: Label and Release Your *Afflictive* Emotions (*Affect*)" (use the emotional crosshairs, quiet waters exercise); "*T*: Observe and Submit Your *Thoughts*" (use the

thinking about your thinking exercise); and "*H*:
Search and Surrender Your *Heart*" (use the openheartedness, spiritual vulnerability exercise).

2) *"e: Engage the World like Christ" practice*: Ultimately,
when you practice holy noticing, you want it to
deepen your relationship with Jesus. Throughout
your day, use the times when you pause to notice,
listen, observe, interact with someone, or check in to
your emotions or thoughts, to remind yourself that
you are God's child, sent to earth to serve and love
Him and to serve and love others. Relish that privi-
lege as you yield to His Spirit's promptings to live in a
God-honoring way.

Bonus material available at www.holynoticing.com/bonus:

• An Ancient Way of Reading God's Word.

• The Boardroom of the Mind Diagram.

Engage the World like Christ

Wherever you are, be all there!
Live to the hilt every situation
you believe to be the will of God.

—JIM ELLIOT, MISSIONARY MARTYRED FOR HIS FAITH

Mindfulness is not primarily about becoming
good at mindfulness practice but, rather, about
becoming a more mindful person in daily life.

—TIM STEAD

JESUS PERFORMED THE MIRACULOUS and never shunned the mundane.

He washed feet, cooked fish, took naps, played with kids, handed out food, and chatted with people in common places and local watering holes alike. He didn't live and serve apart *from* people but *with* people.

He engaged them with gospel living.

As we come to the end of the book, you now understand holy noticing and the BREATHe model, which helps us live more fully in the moment as we become more like Jesus. The last letter of the acronym, *e*, stands for "*Engage* the world like Christ." We may learn the art of holy noticing in the prayer closet, but we practice it in the mundane experiences of life. And if we're honest, much of living for Christ happens in the mundane. The disciples learned that lesson when Jesus told them to go find a donkey (Matt. 21:2).

Sally Welch captures this engaged lifestyle with these words:

> By entering into the moment of these tasks, undertaking them mindfully, aware of every action, taking care over every detail, we can fully inhabit the present. We can relish the task, focusing not only on its results, but on the preparation, offering the moment to God.
>
> "Preparing the way for the Lord" is often made up of performing humble and ordinary tasks—those exhausting, seemingly mundane, donkey-fetching details of service that become, through God's grace, part of the redemptive work of bringing nearer the kingdom of heaven. For even Jesus is not beyond washing feet, sitting by a well, or cooking fish at a lakeside.[1]

Benedict of Nursia founded the Benedictine monastic movement in the sixth century to bring a greater balance to the extreme asceticism some of the early desert fathers and mothers practiced. He summarized his philosophy with this simple phrase: "Pray and work." In other words, those early Christians didn't limit the mindful life to the prayer closet. Rather, they lived out the faith by obeying Jesus' command to love God *and* love their neighbors (Matt. 22:37–39). They understood that you couldn't separate these two commands. Holy noticing ultimately leads us to a more engaged

> **We may learn the art of holy noticing in the prayer closet, but we practice it in the mundane experiences of life.**

life with God and with others, following the pattern of Jesus Himself.

Holy noticing is not a self-serving practice to make us feel better, although being present in the moment does bring greater peace. Rather, it helps release us from unhealthy automatic patterns of thinking, feeling, and relating so that we can direct our energies into productive God-honoring practices and relationships.

Jesus' rebuke to Peter about his pending suffering and death illustrates this: "You do not have in mind the concerns of God, but merely human concerns" (Mark 8:33). Jesus was forcing Peter to make a choice in his thinking, to be mindful of God's perspective rather than his own, which holy noticing helps us do more consistently.

Five Common Obstacles to Engaging the World like Christ

1. Sleepiness. As you learn to be more present and less distracted in your day-to-day life, you may get sleepy. This is quite common, and it doesn't mean you're doing something wrong. It may indicate that you simply need to get more sleep. But even if you are getting enough sleep, sleepiness may still be an obstacle. Choose your most alert time during the day for your formal practice. Mornings work best for most. If you still struggle with sleepiness, practice with your eyes open. Splash cold water on your face. Stand up. Walk around. And if you are a coffee drinker, there's nothing wrong with some extra caffeine.

2. Wandering thoughts and restlessness. You can't avoid wandering thoughts when you practice holy noticing. It's normal. In fact, as you begin to practice, it may seem that your mind wandering has increased. Actually, your practice is revealing what your mind has been doing all along. It's been roaming all over the place. You're just more aware of it now. However, as you practice more, you'll notice more quickly when your mind wanders. When it does, gently bring it back to your breath and the letter of the BREATHe model you were in when it wandered. The more aware you are when your mind wanders, the more progress you're making. I still often thank the Lord for reminders that mine has wandered.

3. *Doubting if this really helps.* Sometimes it's easy to justify skipping your practice. One skip can easily lead to the next and the next and the next until your practice just disappears. I discovered that after the novelty wore off, I struggled and sometimes skipped my practice. At that point I had to remind myself that this was going to benefit my relationship with Jesus, my body and brain, and my relationships with others. After a few weeks, this struggle subsided.

4. *Boredom.* When you're faced with a busy day, it becomes easy to skip your practice. More pressing or interesting tasks may seem like a better use of your time than being quiet and still before God. Again, remind yourself of the benefits you receive from holy noticing. I discovered that the more I practiced, the more interesting it became and boredom was seldom an issue. I now look forward to my daily practice.

5. *Lack of peace.* Holy noticing will bring greater peace to your heart over time. As you learn to meet your troubling thoughts and afflictive emotions with stillness and observation rather than commentary, you will experience peace more often. So, stick with it. You'll move from being a victim of your thoughts and emotions to becoming more like a witness of them. You will still experience some unpleasant ones, but your relationship to them will change. Isaiah paints this picture of

what happen when we're still before God:

The LORD's justice will dwell in the desert,
> his righteousness live in the fertile field.

The fruit of that righteousness will be peace;
> its effect will be quietness and confidence forever.

My people will live in peaceful dwelling places,
> in secure homes,
> in undisturbed places of rest. (32:16–18)

Eight Practical Ways to Engage
the World like Christ through Holy Noticing

1. Recruit some accountability partners. Find a few friends who will encourage you and pray for you to develop holy noticing into a habit. Give them permission to periodically ask you how you're doing.

2. Practice every day, even if only for a minute or so. One minute can easily lead to two minutes and then to three and so on. Practice not only makes perfect but makes permanent. The conventional wisdom that you can build a habit in just twenty-one days isn't true, unfortunately. A recent study showed that it actually takes people an average of sixty-six days to form an enduring, significant new habit.[2] If you want to build this practice into your life, give it a couple of months.[3] As you develop holy-noticing habits, you will move through what is popularly called the four stages of competence. Stage 1 is *unconscious incompetence* when you don't realize the value and benefits of these practices. Stage 2 is *conscious competence* when you realize its value but aren't doing very well with the practice. Stage 3 is *conscious competence* when you begin to apply holy noticing to your life, but it takes conscious effort. And finally stage 4, *unconscious competence,* your ultimate goal, is when it becomes second nature to you.

3. Don't make holy noticing simply another item on your to-do list. View it as an opportunity to daily grow your walk with Jesus and with others. You want this to become a way of life (a trait) rather than simply something you do in your devotional time (a state).

4. Slow down and simply notice. I wrote much of this book on my days off as I sat in the corner booth at a local McDonald's. Some of those days I wrote for twelve hours. I sustained focus by taking mindful walking breaks during the day. I'd often walk by a store in the nearby strip mall that sold potted flowers in the spring and summer. I would often stop to simply notice . . . the flowers, their colors, their shapes, their petals, even down to the tiny filaments inside their blooms. That minute or two pause to notice God's creation invigorated me.

> *Really* listen to others when they speak, and be awake to their words and the simple sounds around you.

Practice holy noticing when you eat, take a shower, walk, wash the dishes, or brush your teeth. Listen when birds chirp, a car horn beeps, when someone laughs, when the wind rustles leaves, when a door closes. *Really* listen to others when they speak, and be awake to their words and the simple sounds around you.

When you eat an apple, for example, think about the food chain and those who got the apple to you. A farmer planted a seed, which grew into a tree, which produced the apple, which was picked by a worker, then was delivered by a trucker, placed in the bin by a produce worker at the grocery store, and then sold to you by a salesperson. As you reflect on all those involved in getting the apple to you, pray for those unseen and unknown people. Eat slowly and really taste your food. Be aware of its texture, crunch, and smell. Thank God for His provision.

When you take Communion, attend to the juice and bread, noting their texture, smell, and taste. Let Communion give you a sense of what the disciples experienced the night before Jesus was crucified.

5. Take mini-moments to notice. I take three-minute mini-moments each day to apply the BREATHe model. I use an app (Time Out) that slowly dims my computer screen every seventy minutes for three minutes (you can search the web to find several similar apps). I close my eyes, take a few deep breaths, pray a few breath prayers, and then briefly touch on each practice in the BREATHe model. I don't always get through all six practices. I trust that the Holy Spirit will prompt me to linger on the one He feels would most benefit me in that moment. Many smart watches also provide similar reminder tools.

6. Practice statio, a cousin to the mini-moments. Statio is an ancient Christian practice that we might call a *mini-transition* between events of the day. It's a moment between moments, when we pause from one task before going to the next. It allows us to break our hurry, obtain closure from the prior task, and prepare our hearts and minds for what comes next. It helps us desire to "do consciously what I might otherwise do mechanically. *Statio* is the virtue of presence."[4] When we practice statio, we can turn down our body's stress accelerator and engage our stress brake, which leads to greater calm.

7. Use the STOP method when you're anxious or worried during the day. This tip is another way to take a mini-moment.

The acronym stands for these four words/phrases: S = Stop, T = Take a breath, O = Observe, and P = Proceed.[5] During the day when something causes you to become anxious, literally stop what you're doing. Take a few slow, deep breaths. Observe and acknowledge your distressing emotions and thoughts without adding commentary. Then move on.

8. *Schedule a few minutes a day for at least five days a week to practice.* I schedule my devotional time in the mornings and incorporate fifteen to twenty minutes of practice into those devotions. You may want to start with five to ten minutes and build up. Most experts say that if you practice for twenty minutes, five days a week, you will see significant, long-lasting results in three to four months, especially with stress management.[6]

The apostle Paul reminds us that growing is a progressive process when he wrote, "I have learned to be content" (Phil. 4:11). It took time and experience for him to *learn* contentment. The more experience he had, the more he learned contentment. The same is true for the effects of mindful living. As you build these practices into your daily life, you will experience more benefits. If you can't do twenty minutes at a time, at least be consistent in practicing each day. Even shorter practice periods can help.[7]

I began this book with the story about the brain tumor diagnosis that our youngest daughter, Tiffany, received at age one. That began my journey of learning about holy noticing, a mindful lifestyle.

During one stay at Johns Hopkins Hospital when Tiffany was five and recovering from her third brain surgery, a profound experience left an impression I can still visualize with crystal clarity.

A few days after her surgery, the doctor allowed me to wheel Tiffany around the hospital in a kid-sized wheelchair. It was the Christmas season, and a nurse suggested I take her to the hospital rotunda to see the holiday decorations. So we took the elevator to the first floor, and after navigating a few hospital hallways, we entered the huge rotunda.

In the center stood a twelve-foot marble statue of Jesus with nail-pierced hands outstretched. Dozens of red poinsettas formed a pyramid at the base of the statue. Tiffany was dressed in a white ankle-length gown. Red zig-zag trim wrapped her sleeves. Five tiny silver buttons cascaded down the front of her gown. Her head was tightly wrapped in gauze. My wife had gingerly attached a small red bow on the gauze to hide the blood that had stained it.

As I wheeled her in, my eyes and ears were immediately drawn to the second-floor balcony that surrounded the rotunda. A dozen college-aged singers stood there. At the very moment we entered, the students began to sing an a cappella rendition of "O Holy Night."

I tightened my hands around the wheelchair handles to distract myself. I was trying to avoid shedding tears in a public place. But the singers' perfect pitch, the echo in the rotunda, the words of the song itself, and the statue of Jesus all combined to create a holy moment for me and my daughter.

Then she started to bound over to us. A girl with red hair in pigtails.

Perhaps fifty feet to my right, a social worker had led a group of young patients into the rotunda to hear the music. These kids were obviously very sick, and their parents were not with them.

This young girl with the red pigtails had broken rank and

was literally running over to Tiffany. They were about the same age. Without a shred of self-consciousness, she put a hand on each of Tiffany's hands and asked, "Why are you in the hospital?" They began to chat. This little girl intently listened as Tiffany explained her brain surgery.

She then carefully touched the bow on her head.

And lovingly stroked Tiffany's arm.

And smiled.

And ran back to her line of friends.

My hands tightened around the handles even more.

In those two minutes my heart was struck by this pure, diminutive "noticer."

She didn't know me.

We didn't know her.

But she gave me a lesson in holy noticing I will never forget.

Little girl with red pigtails, thank you for noticing Tiffany that day when my heart was so heavy.

You touched my soul.

Without knowing it, you modeled for me what it means to be a holy noticer.

Your simple act of noticing Tiffany helped propel me into a life-changing journey.

I will never forget it.

I will never forget you.

Thank you for helping me become a holy noticer.

A Full BREATHe Session

IN THIS APPENDIX, I'VE COMBINED all the practices into one session of the BREATHe model so you can see what it might look like to incorporate it all at once into your devotional time. Keep these tips in mind, just as you have when you've tried each practice individually.

1. Find a comfortable place in your home that is quiet, undisturbed, and free from distractions. But don't get too comfortable. Choose a chair that supports your back and sit up straight.

2. Have your Bible with you to refer to your anchor verses if you've not memorized them. You can also use the downloadable tool that includes the practices, anchor verses, visual metaphors, and skills for the entire BREATHe model. Find it at www.holynoticing.com.

3. I recommend closing your eyes to block visual distractions. If you get sleepy, it's okay to open them. You also may want to open them when you practice the *E*.

4. Set your timer. Twenty minutes works well for me. You may want to start with less time, and that's okay. The key is consistency. If your timer goes off but you haven't finished and want to keep going a few minutes longer, that's fine.

5. Don't get frustrated when your mind wanders. It will. When you become aware that it has, thank the Lord for reminding you. Simply refocus on your breath by taking a couple of slow, deep breaths while you repeat your breath prayer. Then silently ask yourself, *Now where was I?* B . . . R . . . E . . . *oh yeah,* E. *That's where I was, on* E, *the environment.*

6. Seek to make holy noticing a trait of your life, not simply an add-on to your devotional life. Practice being in the moment in your day-to-day routine. If you're diligent, you will experience tangible benefits.

B: Ponder and Yield Your *Body*
Anchor verses: Psalm 139:14; 1 Corinthians 6:19–20; Romans 12:1

[Begin with long, slow breaths.
Breathe in.
Breathe out.
Breathe in.
Breathe out.
Breathe in and breathe out with your breath prayer.]

Holy Spirit [the in-breath]
Breathe on me [the out-breath]

[Repeat your breath prayer as long as you want. You may want to include other breath prayers such as *Lord Jesus* (on the in-breath) *You are good* (on the out-breath).]
[Move on to your anchor verses for *B*.]

Lord, I come before You and present my body to You. I want to ponder it and yield it to You right now.

[Meditate on your anchor verses, or read them if you have not memorized them.]

Lord, I acknowledge that I am fearfully and wonderfully made. I know that full well.
I acknowledge that my body is a temple of the Holy Spirit that You have freely given to me.
I am not my own. I have been bought with a price.
I want to honor You with my body.
Therefore, I now offer my body as a living sacrifice to You.

[Begin your body scan. Start with your left foot and leg as you imagine a scanner passing over it from bottom to top. Pause at various places to feel any sensation, no sensation, or sensations that come and go. Focus your attention on that part of your body. Notice how sensations may change. Thank God for that part of your body. Be creative in what you thank Him for. You may thank Him for such things as how your knee flexes, for your kneecap, or for the cartilage and ligaments that hold your knee together.

Now move to your right leg and do the same, noticing sensations that come and go. Thank God at various places on your leg.

Move to your torso and then up your left hand and arm and up your right hand and arm. Thank God at various places in your torso and hands and arms.

Now move up your neck, up your face, and finally up through your head. You may thank Him for things that seem insignificant, such as your eyelashes or the contours of your ear. Remember, God has fashioned you as the crown of His creation.

Simply notice and express thanks. You are here to be with your body in the presence of the One who created it. Sometimes you may want to revisit your anchor verses during your body scan. That's fine. When your timer sounds, you can stop, even if you haven't scanned your entire body. If you want to, you can keep going after your timer sounds. Close with these prayers.]

*Lord, thank You for giving me my body. I am fearfully and
wonderfully made.*
I yield it to You today as a living sacrifice.

Transition to *R*: Review and Renew Your *Relationships*
Anchor verses: John 13:34–35

[Move on to your anchor verses for *R*. Meditate on them by reading or reciting them from memory.]

*Lord, I bring my relationships before You. I want to review and renew
them as Your Spirit guides.*
Please give me a sense of Your grace right now.
Show me Your love.
Help me love others as You have loved me.

[Now visualize those in your concentric circles. Start in the center circle
with those closest to you. Ask questions like these.]

How are things in this relationship?
Is this relationship healthy?
Is there some work I need to do?
Is there something regarding this relationship I should be praying about?
Do I need to confess a bad attitude toward this person?

[Linger a bit with the image of that person in your mind. Pray for them
as the Spirit prompts. Then move to the next person in your concentric
circles diagram, and so on. Don't feel as though you need to cover every
relationship. God will bring to mind those you need to focus on today. If
you get stuck on a person who invokes a negative response, move on. The
deeper the hurt, the longer it will take to heal and wish this person well.]

Lord, thank You for putting these people in my circle of relationships.
I recommit them to You.
Help me refresh and renew these relationships on an ongoing basis.
If I must interact with a difficult person today, give me Your grace to
respond in a godly way.

Transition to *E*: Notice and Engage Your *Environment*
Anchor verses: Psalm 8; Psalm 95:4–5

[Move on to your anchor verses for *E*. Meditate on them by reading or
reciting them from memory.]

Lord, I bring my attention to the environment You have placed me in
right now.
Thank You
. . . for the ability to hear
. . . for the air I breathe
. . . for Your magnificent creation
. . . for the sounds that surround me right now.

[Imagine you are sending a sonar "ping" into your surroundings. Listen deeply to the sounds you hear. Is it the air-conditioning, the clock, the wind outside (or the wind blowing in the trees if you are outside), birds chirping, a neighbor's lawn mower, stirrings of your family members in your home?

Listen for whatever comes your way.

Catch yourself if you begin to add commentary, and refocus on the sound.

Just listen to the tone, timber, beat, and so on of the sounds. Remember, you are strengthening your attentional muscles with this skill.

You may want to then try focused observation.

Open your eyes and focus on an object that you've not focused on before, such as the flower in the windowsill, the lampshade, the sofa, familiar objects you may have taken for granted. What new things do you notice that you've never seen before? Is it a color, a pattern, or an unusual aspect of that object?

If you are at a window or outside, focus your attention on a tree branch, a leaf, a flower petal, or something else in nature. Notice its shape, color, size, uniqueness, symmetry or asymmetry.

Revel in God's creation.

Remember, you are simply noticing, not adding commentary.]

Lord, I thank You for the senses You've given me to enjoy Your
creation.
Hone my attentional skills.

*Help me become a better "holy noticer" of You, Your creation,
and others.*

Transition to *A*: Label and
Release Your *Afflictive* Emotions *(Affect)*
Anchor verses: Galatians 5:22–23

[Move on to your anchor verses for A. Meditate on them by slowly reading or reciting them from memory. If you are using Galatians 5:22–23
as your anchor verses, reflect on each quality mentioned. Visualize in
your mind someone you know or yourself demonstrating love, joy, peace,
and so on. Remember, you're in no rush. Take your time. And when your
mind wanders, which it will, thank God for helping you recognize it. Don't
berate yourself for a wandering mind. Simply refocus on your breath and
pick up where you left off.]

*Lord, I pause right now to be present with You and my affect, my
emotions, both pleasant and afflictive ones.*
*I want to relate to any difficult emotions in a way that honors You and
helps me release them to You.*
*I don't want to push them away but to acknowledge their existence
even as I know Your Spirit is with me right now.*
Lord, reveal to me any afflictive emotions right now.
I'm having feelings of _____

_____.

[Label and describe how you feel, both good and bad emotions. Use the crosshairs exercise or Rifle Scope Chart if you need help. Remember, when we label our difficult emotions, their power over us decreases. Simply name and describe them without adding commentary or judgment. Observe them without getting caught up in them or judging them as right or wrong. Remind yourself that these emotions don't define you. You aren't ascribing intent to them or evaluating them. You are simply observing them as transient passing mental events. Try to use descriptive words (i.e., *unfortunate*) rather than evaluative words (i.e., *horrible*).]

Lord, I am noticing the emotion of (anger, etc.) right now.
I acknowledge it without pushing it away.
My (anger) does not pose a threat to me. I am safe in Your care.

[Stay aware of your tendency to push away, suppress, or use the Whac-A-Mole strategy.

If you sense sin behind the emotion, confess it. But remember that feeling does not automatically imply sin.

Once you've labeled them, it's time to release these emotions to the Lord. Turn your attention to skill 2, the quiet waters exercise from Psalm 23.]

Lord, I release my (anger, etc.) to You.
I let go of it.
May Your Spirit now grow in me greater love, joy, peace, patience,
kindness, goodness, faithfulness, gentleness, and self-control so that
I don't try to suppress my emotions or let them control me.
Thank You, Lord, for helping me.

Transition to *T*: Observe and Submit Your *Thoughts*
Anchor verses: 2 Corinthians 10:5;
Romans 12:2; Philippians 4:8; Isaiah 26:3

[Move on to your anchor verses. Meditate on them by reading or reciting them from memory.]

Lord, I submit my thoughts to You right now.
Help me sort through which thoughts are true and correct and
which are not.
Help me be with my thoughts without adding commentary to them.

[As thoughts rise up in your mind, try to reframe troublesome ones such as *I am anxious* to a decentered thought such as *I am having feelings of anxiety*, which provokes less anxiety. By labeling thoughts in this way, you're adding some distance between them and their effects on you. Other phrases could include, *I am having memories of . . . , feelings that . . . , thoughts about . . . , bodily sensations of . . .* , and so on.

Try to simply name your thought instead of spinning a commentary about it. Remember, you are developing the skill of thinking about your thinking (metacognition), the ability to think about your own mental state. As you grow in a holy-noticing lifestyle, you'll get better at this.[1] One helpful way to distance yourself from your unhealthy thoughts is to learn to differentiate between a description and an evaluation. A description is just that, a description of an event or an emotion. An evaluation attributes subjective qualities to an event. For example, a description would be: "I am having feelings of fear." An evaluation would be: "My fear is intolerable." Evaluations often intensify our emotions.

Imagine that you are on a mountain and are observing the weather. You are secure in the Lord, and your difficult thoughts are like the weather. View those thoughts as passing storms.]

Lord, I submit this thought to You: [fill in the blank]
And this one . . .
And this one . . .
Help me be present with these thoughts.
Thank You that I am not my thoughts.
I am as secure as Mount Zion. You are my rock, my fortress, my strength, my truth.

[Here you may want to recall and reflect on your anchor verses again. There is no need to try to dredge up negative thoughts. As thoughts arise, even good ones, be present with them. If thoughts arise that are potentially sinful, bring those before the Holy Spirit and let Him bring appropriate conviction. Confess those that He convicts you are sinful.]

Lord, help me live out the reality of having the mind of Christ.
I want to think thoughts that honor You.
I submit my thinking to You.

Transition to *H*: Search and Surrender Your *Heart*
Anchor verses: Psalm 139:23–24; Zephaniah 3:17

[Move on to your anchor verses. Meditate on them by reading or reciting them from memory.]

Lord, I yield my heart to You right now.
Please shine Your searchlight on my soul.

[Envision a bright searchlight shining on your heart.]

Reveal to me any hidden sin or wrong attitudes.

[Pause and simply be still before the Lord.
As God reveals sin, respond with confession.
After a few moments, reflect on Zephaniah 3:17 or Scriptures that clarify your position and identity in Christ.]

Lord, I rejoice in the fact that You rejoice and sing over me.
I receive Your affirmations of my identity and position in Christ.

[One way to experience this is to recall times when you felt truly loved by others. Recall the details of those experiences. You may want to write them down.

You may want to list your strengths and thank God for them. Beware of any tendency to criticize yourself or bring up your flaws. Remember, God takes great delight in you and rejoices over you. He loves you with an everlasting love.]

Lord, thank You for Your love, mercy, care, and concern for me.
I receive it with gratefulness.

[end of the practice when your timer goes off at eighteen to twenty minutes]

How Holy Noticing Affects Your Brain

I used to think that the brain was the most wonderful
organ in my body. Then I realized who was telling me this.
—EMO PHILIPS

YOUR PARENTS OR A SCHOOLTEACHER probably taught you about about the birds and the bees. But did you ever get a talk from them about your brain? Probably not. Yet this walnut-shaped, tofu-textured, cantaloupe-sized powerhouse profoundly affects every part of your life, including your spiritual life. And holy noticing can create positive changes in your brain. In this chapter I give a simple bird's-eye view of the brain and its basic functions, especially as it relates to how mindfulness affects it.

In Psalm 139, King David muses and marvels over God's handiwork in the human body. He says in verse 14, "I am fearfully and wonderfully made; your works are wonderful." If he lived today and knew what scientists now know about the brain, I'm sure he'd echo the same sentiment about our brains.

Composed of between eighty-six and one hundred billion neurons (plus other kinds of cells), with connections estimated to exceed the number of stars in the universe, the human brain weighs a mere 2–3 percent of the average body's weight, yet consumes almost 20 percent of our body's energy. It's so complex that it would take thousands of books to begin to plumb its complexity.

As we learn about the brain, it's helpful to understand the interplay of faith and science. As psychiatrist Matthew Stafford writes,

> God's majesty is reflected in how our brain cells function, the biological and environmental factors that affect the formation of our personalities, the mechanism by which memories are brought to our minds, and the precise balance of brain chemicals that are the foundation of our thoughts and behaviors.[1]

And John Polkinghorne, a Christian who was the former professor of mathematical physics at Cambridge University, wrote, "Science and theology have things to say to each other since both are concerned with the search for truth attained through motivated belief."[2]

Throughout history, science and religion have related to each other in one of four ways: conflict, independence (they both keep their distance from each other), dialogue (even after meaningful dialogue, each side retreats into its own framework), and integration (collaborative, bidirectional, and reciprocal learning).[3] In this book I've taken the fourth approach, believing that since good neuroscience is God's truth, we can learn from it. And, there is a growing movement of intellectuals who, although may not be Christian, are embracing the reality of the supernatural.[4]

How Your Brain Works

Just as a house includes multiple components—rooms, building materials such as bricks, systems such as plumbing, Wi-Fi, and electrical—our brains are made up of several parts called lobes. The brain's main building components are called neurons (brain cells), along with other kinds of cells, primarily glia cells, and its systems are called neural networks.

God fashioned our brains in two mirror-image halves, like a walnut, with the sides joined by a superhighway of neural connections called the corpus callosum. Each hemisphere includes five major rooms or lobes—occipital, parietal, temporal, frontal, and insular. And scientists generally agree that four *major* networks form the brain (there are many minor ones as well)—the visual network, the salience network (makes things stand out in importance), the attentional network, and the default mode network (the circuit that activates when we aren't focused on a task and are thinking mostly about ourselves and what we believe others are thinking about us). Generally speaking, circuits in our brains (like a bunch of computers networked together) either receive information, perceive information, or conceive information. Here's a simple diagram of the brain with its basic functions.

CORTICAL LOBES

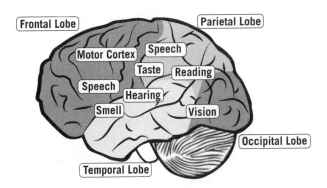

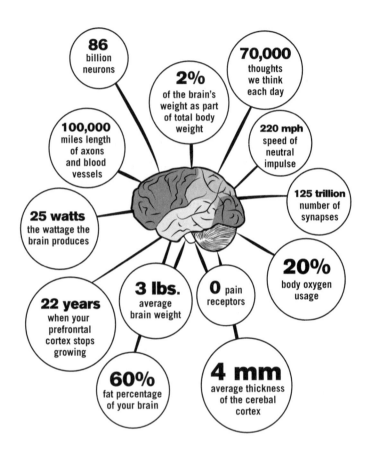

Different functions are generally localized (located in one area of the brain), but neuroscientists are discovering that the brain's functions are much more distributed than once thought. The left side of the brain is more linear, logical, and linguistic (sees the trees), and the right side is more artistic and wholistic (sees the forest). The left side tends to explain things more (the left bone is connected to the right bone), and the right side tends to describe things more (I am so sad that my bones ache).

An overriding principle guides our brain: Minimize Danger/Threat—Maximize Reward/Pleasure. The terms *away* and *toward* correspond to danger/threat and reward/pleasure. Although many brain parts are involved in and affected by mindful practice, it's helpful to know a few most impacted.

Our executive center, the brain's CEO, is called the prefrontal cortex and is located behind our forehead and temples. The acronym REAP describes what our brains' CEO does: **R**ational thinking (planning, analyzing, goal setting, insight, morality); **E**motional regulation; **A**ttention; and **P**eople (how we perceive and relate to others).

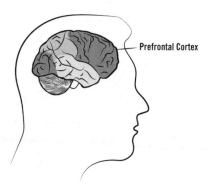

The middle part (which stretches from between our eyes and traverses all the way to the back of our head—think of a Mohawk), helps us understand how present experiences relate to our past and how they may affect our future. This part is activated when we pay attention to ourselves and when we think about what others may be thinking about us. It gives us a sense of self and activates when we're not focused on a task. It's called the *default mode network* (DMN). Holy noticing helps us keep that network in check when we tend to worry and get anxious and it also influences that network to increase creativity.[5]

Our limbic system, what neuroscientist Jeffrey Schwartz calls our "Uh Oh Center"[6] is the fight/flight/freeze system (our feeler), which includes four major brain parts, each with a particular function. The hypothalamus affects our response to stress. The amygdala (there are two of them and two of every part of our brains) is an almond-shaped cluster of neurons that revs up fear, anxiety, and other unpleasant emotions when we feel threatened. The hippocampus is a seahorse-shaped cluster of neurons involved in creating memories. It helps us remember the names of our coworkers while the amygdala reminds us who we do and don't like. And finally, the cingulate cortex, which lies between our CEO and our emotional centers and right above the superhighway that connects both sides of the brain (corpus collosum), influences attention and focus and acts like a mediator between thinking and feeling. The front part of the cingulate cortex (the anterior cingulate cortex) is a conflict monitor, alerting us when our goals, preferences, and beliefs are in conflict with our actions. It's like a smoke detector that alerts us when something isn't right.

Another brain region influenced by this practice is the insula. Located deep within the brain, it enables us to experience our internal body sensations (called interoception) and their salience. *Salience* is a term to describe how worthy those sensations are of our attention (chunky chocolate triple fudge peanut butter ice cream is more salient than a radish). The insula is also involved in intuition, our "gut" feeling.

What Holy Noticing Does to Your Brain

A key impact from mindfulness practice involves our inner body states. Holy noticing helps us become more aware of those inner body states because it helps strengthen the connections between the brain's CEO and the insula.[7] It also helps hone our ability to sense and understand those internal body states because the practice activates the insula.[8]

When our thinking gets negative (the tendency of our default mode network, the Mohawk), holy noticing can give us stronger and quicker access to the brain's direct mode (what the brain does when we focus on a task). This helps minimize the effects of negative thinking. It decreases mind wandering,[9] which usually defaults to negative thinking. It also strengthens the neural pathways between our CEO and our feeler (amygdala), which helps us control negative emotions.[10] And, as one author writes, "Over time this increases our capacity to focus so that we can more intentionally allow God's Spirit to direct our thoughts and control our emotions. This is why Scripture says we are transformed by the renewing of our minds (Romans 12:2). In essence . . . we are aligning our brains with the work the Holy Spirit is doing in our hearts."[11]

Your brain's chemical messengers (neurotransmitters)

Most neurons are programmed to produce, send, and receive certain chemicals called neurotransmitters—chemical messengers that relay information from one neuron to the next. Think of a courier relaying information from one person to the next. These chemicals activate the next brain cell (called excitatory) or keep it from firing (called inhibitory). The amount of these chemicals affects our well-being, happiness, and our spiritual health. Sometimes these chemicals become imbalanced with too much or too little of them. And, a mindful lifestyle is implicated in increasing the levels of several important brain chemicals.[12]

- *Dopamine* is involved in reward, wanting, motivation, attention, and learning. Too much or too little of this one can inhibit attention, create addictions, and cause fatigue.

- *Acetylcholine* affects how fast your brain processes data, acting somewhat like a lubricant to keep energy and information flowing well. A lack of this one creates brain fog.

- *GABA* (short for a really long word) is involved in producing the feel-good hormones we experience in exercise and sex. An imbalance leads to anxiety.

- *Serotonin* is involved in healing, mood, good sleep, and the sense of feeling satisfied. When this one gets out of balance, we get depressed and don't sleep well.[13]

Dopamine and acetylcholine are like the brain's "on" switches to give us energy. GABA and serotonin are like the brain's "off" switches to help calm us. Mindful practice also apparently increases the neurotransmitter called oxytocin that builds trust between people.[14] "It seems that oxytocin makes our neuronal pathways more malleable, enabling us to learn—and unlearn—more readily than we normally would. We become more impressionable; as a result, change becomes easier."[15]

Eight Amazing Facts about Holy Noticing and Your Brain That Will Blow Your Mind (Maybe)

1. *It physically changes your brain.* Neuroscientist Andrew Newberg studied a group of nuns who had been practicing a form of holy noticing, centering prayer, for at least fifteen years. He discovered significant neurological changes in their brains.[16] In another study, after participants completed an eight-week course and practiced it for an average of twenty-seven minutes a day, their brains got thicker in these regions: areas involving mind wandering, learning, emotional regulation, empathy, and compassion. And, their brains shrunk in the regions of fear, anxiety, and stress.[17]

2. *You can shape your brain with your thoughts.*[18] Related to number 1, this process is called *experience dependent neuroplasticity.* Another term, *competitive neuroplasticity*, describes the brain's tendency to look for neglected neurons to recruit for new purposes. The adage "Use or it lose it" applies to your brain as well. If you want to retain your brain cells, you must use them, because our thoughts and experiences actually reshape the brain's wiring. The more you think about something (i.e., reflect on the truth in Scripture), the more your brain allocates its real estate to the subject of those thoughts. It forges stronger connections to other parts of the brain. The opposite holds true as well. If you repeatedly focus your thoughts on negative experiences (i.e., my friend hurt me with her words), those negative thoughts get wired more deeply into your brain. What you think about changes your brain. Our mental habits, to what we give our attention, literally shape our brains, which in turn shape our behavior. This relates to the biblical concept of "renewing . . . your mind" (Rom. 12:2).

3. *You can grow new brain cells even into old age.* At one time neuroscientists believed that once we got past our teen years, the brain was fixed and couldn't grow any more brain cells. However, recent research shows that we *can* grow new brain cells, especially in our memory centers (the hippocampus). The process is called neurogenesis.[19]

4. *Your brain is hardwired to be negative, and holy noticing combats negative thinking. Negativity bias* is a term that explains that we are hardwired and primed to detect and pick up on negative information more easily than positive information. This is one of the effects from the fall in the garden of Eden. We recall negative things more quickly, mentally and emotionally imprint negative things more easily than positive ones, tend to make things gloomier than they are (called mood bias), and remember negative experiences longer than positive ones. At the same time, this bias causes us to downplay life's positive experiences. One expert says that our brains are like "Velcro for negative experiences and Teflon for positive ones—even though most of our experiences are probably neutral or positive."[20] Yet holy noticing helps us notice this natural tendency so that we can change how we think. The apostle Paul understood this tendency and reminded us to let our minds dwell on that which is good and wholesome (see Phil. 4:8).

5. *Your brain wanders almost 50 percent of the time.* The *default mode network* (referred to above) describes the state our minds drift to when we aren't directly focused on a task (called the *direct mode*). The default mode activates when we think about ourselves and how we think others think about us, often leading to unhappy thoughts. Mindful practice helps decrease mind wandering and helps us become more aware of it because it strengthens the connections between our thinking

centers and the brain circuits in the default mode network. As a result, we gain more control over mind wandering.[21]

Jesus taught us to seek first His kingdom and to put others first (see Matt. 6:33). Holy noticing helps us do this because it decreases self-focused thinking. Also, the apostle Paul instructed us to set our minds on things above (Col. 3:1). As we intentionally place our attention on these areas, our brains disengage from the default mode. On the other hand, since the default mode causes self-preoccupation, it usually magnifies unhappiness.

But not all mind wandering is unhealthy. Psychologist Jerome L. Singer[22] classifies mind wandering into three categories: (1) poor attention control (we can't stay focused on important tasks); (2) guilty-dysphoric (when our mind wanders to guilt, anxiety, and angry situations); and (3) positive-constructive. Mind wandering benefits us when we envision future possibilities, set goals (called prospective bias), or think about creative solutions to problems we face.

6. *It may actually make you smarter.* Mindfulness has been shown to increase the amount of the brain's gray matter (neurons make up gray matter), thicken the insulation (myelin) around the tail of a brain cell (the axon), thicken the axon itself,[23] and strengthen the circuits between the brain's error detector (the anterior cingulate cortex) and the pleasure center (the nucleus accumbens).

More gray matter means more available circuitry to process information. More myelin and thicker axons mean you can process things more quickly. And greater connectivity improves self-control, planning, and attention.

7. *You can read other people's minds (kind of).* A category of neurons called mirror neurons acts like your brain's virtual

reality simulation center. These neurons are involved in mentalizing (the process called theory of mind). It's the ability to resonate with the feelings and intentions of others by feeling your own. We might call it intuition or discernment.

In biblical days, pagan and Jewish mystics and prophets would claim special revelation. John cautioned his readers to "test the spirits to see whether they are from God" (1 John 4:1). The same holds true for us today. We must test not only what we hear others tell us but also the thoughts that we tell ourselves in our unspoken self-talk. When our "theory of mind" is poorly tuned, we can misinterpret the motives and intents of others, which can wreak havoc in our minds and relationships. Mindful practice helps hone our ability to accurately sense the emotional states of others.

8. *It helps you become more comfortable in your own skin, with your own thoughts.* Most people prefer to not be alone with their thoughts. In one study referred to earlier in the book, participants chose to give themselves mild to moderate electrical shocks rather than sitting by themselves in a room for fifteen minutes with nothing to do except be with their thoughts. One-third of the men and one-fourth of the women were so uncomfortable with their thoughts that they preferred a distraction, even if it meant the shock. One participant shocked himself 190 times. A mindful lifestyle, however, can help us become more comfortable with our thoughts and emotions, and less likely to stuff or ignore them.[24]

Acknowledgments

THIS BOOK WOULD NOT HAVE been possible without the influence of many special people.

First of all, I deeply appreciate the unending support from my wife, Sherryl. She has encouraged me to write and has helped me persevere when the words sometimes wouldn't come. My three children, Heather, Josh, and Tiffany, have given me much joy as well and made my writing richer.

My initial editor, Ingrid Beck, set the book on a good trajectory. My main editor, Connor Sterchi, continued to amaze me with his attention to detail and constructive editorial suggestions. And I was extremely honored to have Moody's editorial director, Randall Payleitner, take a keen interest in the book with his insightful suggestions. Ashley Torres, Moody's book marketing manager, has brought her quality experience in marketing to maximize the book's reach. And to all the staff at Moody working behind the scenes, thanks so much. It's an honor to be an author for Moody.

Steve Laube has wisely guided me through my writing career with his sage and candid advice, serving as my agent for all five of my books. He has helped me navigate the challenges of writing and publishing.

I must also include the gracious people in London, Ontario at the church where I pastor, West Park Church. They have graciously listened to me as I wove brain insight into my teaching and my leadership.

And, finally, I want to thank my savior, Jesus Christ, who paid the ultimate price for me through His sacrificial work on the cross and resurrection.

Notes

Introduction: The Spiritual and Practical Benefits of Holy Noticing

1. Sally Welch, *How to Be a Mindful Christian: 40 Simple Spiritual Practices* (Norwich, UK: Canterbury Press, 2016), loc. 124, Kindle.
2. Mark Williams and Danny Penman, *Mindfulness: An Eight-Week Plan for Finding Peace in a Frantic World* (New York: Rodale, 2012), loc. 539, Kindle.
3. Elizabeth Harrington, "NIH Has Spent $100.2 Million on Mindfulness Meditation," *Washington Free Beacon*, December 16, 2014, http://freebeacon.com/issues/ nih-has-spent-92-9-million-on-mindfulness-meditation.
4. J en Wieczner, "Meditation Has Become a Billion-Dollar Business," *Fortune*, March 12, 2016, http://fortune.com/2016/03/12/ meditation-mindfulness-apps.
5. Kif Leswing, "Apple Just Named Its Favorite Apps and Games of the Year," December 7, 2017, www.businessinsider.com/ apple-iphone-ipad-app-of-the-year-for-2017-12.
6. Shaun Lambert, *Putting on the Wakeful One: Attuning to the Spirit of Jesus through Watchfulness* (Watford, UK: Instant Apostle, 2016), loc. 771–72, Kindle.
7. J. I. Packer, *Knowing God* (Downers Grove, IL: IVP Books, 2011), 23.
8. Albrecht Wattimury, *Billy Graham—I'd Spend More Time in Meditation and Prayer*, March 14, 2013, YouTube video, 2:27, www. youtube.com/watch?v=2dIuWwQAOTo.
9. Alex Pattakos and Elaine Dundon, *Prisoners of Our Thoughts: Viktor Frankl's Principles for Discovering Meaning in Life and Work*, 3rd ed. (Oakland, CA: Berrett-Koehler Publishers, 2017), x.
10. Welch, *How to Be a Mindful Christian*, loc. 129.
11. Kirk Warren Brown, J. David Creswell, and Richard M. Ryan, eds., *Handbook of Mindfulness: Theory, Research, and Practice* (Plymouth, UK: Guilford Press, 2015), 329.
12. Ernest E. Larkin, "Christian Mindfulness," n.d., http://carmelnet. org/larkin/larkin017.pdf, 6.
13. Shaun Lambert, *A Book of Sparks: A Study in Christian MindFullness* (Watford, UK: Instant Apostle, 2014), loc. 347, Kindle.
14. Joanna Collicutt and Roger Bretherton, *Being Mindful, Being Christian: A Guide to Mindful Discipleship* (Monarch Books, 2016), loc. 204, Kindle.
15. G. E. H. Palmer, Philip Sherrard, and Bishop Kallistos Ware, trans., *Philokalia—The Eastern Christian Spiritual Texts: Selections Annotated and Explained* (Woodstock, VT: SkyLight Paths, 2012), loc. 2480, Kindle.
16. Tim Stead, *Mindfulness and Christian Spirituality: Making Space for God* (London, UK: SPCK, 2016), loc. 372, Kindle.

17. Stefan Reynolds, "Why Practising Christian Mindfulness Doesn't Mean Turning Buddhist," Christian Today, October 25, 2016, www.christiantoday.com/article/why.practising.christian.mindfulness.doesnt.mean.turning.buddhist/98510.htm.

18. Fernando Garzon, *Christian Devotional Meditation for Anxiety: Chapter 4, Evidence-Based Practices for Christian Counseling and Psychotherapy*, ed. Everett L. Worthington et al. (Downers Grove, IL: IVP Academic, 2016), loc. 44, Kindle.

19. Collicutt and Bretherton, *Being Mindful*, loc. 701.

20. Stead, *Mindfulness and Christian Spirituality*, loc. 813 .

21. Collicutt and Bretherton, *Being Mindful*, loc. 491.

22. Jack Kornfield, *A Lamp in the Darkness: Illuminating the Path through Difficult Times* (Boulder, CO: Sounds True, 2014), 7.

23. Timothy Keller, *Prayer: Experiencing Awe and Intimacy with God* (New York: Penguin Books, 2014), loc. 216, Kindle; quotes within quote from Thomas R. Schreiner, *Romans: Baker Exegetical Commentary on the New Testament* (Marietta, GA: Baker, 1998), 427.

24. John Jefferson Davis, *Meditation and Communion with God: Contemplating Scripture in an Age of Distraction* (Downers Grove, IL: IVP Academic, 2012), loc. 337, Kindle.

25. Mark A. Noll, *Jesus Christ and the Life of the Mind* (Grand Rapids, MI: Eerdmans, 2011), ix–x.

26. Collicutt and Bretherton, *Being Mindful*, loc. 256.

27. Susan L. Smalley and Diana Winston, *Fully Present: The Science, Art, and Practice of Mindfulness* (Boston: Da Capo Press, 2010), loc. 408, Kindle.

28. Stead, *Mindfulness and Christian Spirituality,* loc. 496.

Chapter 1: What Mindfulness Is, What It's Not, and Why It Matters

1. Kirk A. Bingaman, *The Power of Neuroplasticity for Pastoral and Spiritual Care* (Lanham, MD: Lexington Books, 2014), loc. 115, Kindle.

2. Kirk D. Strosahl and Patricia J. Robinson, *In This Moment: Five Steps to Transcending Stress Using Mindfulness and Neuroscience*, (Oakland, CA: New Harbinger Publications, 2015), 66–67.

3. Jon Kabat-Zinn, *Mindfulness for Beginners: Reclaiming the Present Moment and Your Life* (Boulder, CO: Sounds True, 2016), loc. 353–1517, Kindle.

4. Reynolds, *Living with the Mind of Christ,* loc. 262.

5. This is called affective bias.

6. This is called knowing wrongly. Kirk Warren Brown, J. David Creswell, and Richard M. Ryan, eds., *Handbook of Mindfulness: Theory, Research, and Practice* (Plymouth, UK: Guilford Press, 2015).

7. This is called interoception. "The Strange Case of Interoception and Resilience or How to Become a Superhero," *Body in Mind* (blog), May 17, 2016, www.bodyinmind.org/interoception-resilience.

8. This is called metacognition. Dilwar Hussain, "Meta-Cognition in Mindfulness: A Conceptual Analysis," *Psychological Thought* 8, no. 2 (October 16, 2015): 132–41.

9. This is called de-centering.

10. Sonja Lyubomirsky, *The How of Happiness: A New Approach to Getting the Life You Want* (New York: Penguin Books, 2007), 64.

11. Richard J. Davidson et al., "Alterations in Brain and Immune Function Produced by Mindfulness Meditation," *Psychosomatic Medicine* 65, no. 4 (August 2003): 564–70.

12. Thomas G. Szabo et al., "Mindfulness in Contextual Cognitive-Behavioral Models," in *Handbook of Mindfulness: Theory, Research, and Practice*, ed. Brown, Creswell, and Ryan, 133.

13. J. David Creswell et al., "Neural Correlates of Dispositional Mindfulness During Affect Labeling," *Psychosomatic Medicine* 69, no. 6 (July 2007): 560–65, https://doi.org/10.1097/PSY.0b013e3180f6171f.

14. Oswald Chambers, *My Utmost for His Highest*, rev. ed., ed. James Reimann (Grand Rapids, MI: Discovery House Publishers, 2010), 275.

15. Ibid., 276.

Chapter 2: How the Bible and Church History Support This Ancient Spiritual Discipline

1. Scott Barry Kaufman and Carolyn Gregoire, *Wired to Create: Unraveling the Mysteries of the Creative Mind* (New York: TarcherPerigee, 2015), 103.

2. Ronald D. Siegel, Andrew Olendzki, and Christopher K. Germer, "Mindfulness: What Is It? Where Does It Come From?," in *Clinical Handbook of Mindfulness* (New York: Springer, 2008), 26,

3. "Zakar," Bible Study Tools, www.biblestudytools.com/lexicons/hebrew/nas/zakar.html.

4. Stefan Gillow Reynolds, *Living with the Mind of Christ: Mindfulness in Christian Spirituality* (London: Darton, Longman and Todd Ltd, 2016), loc. 796, Kindle.

5. Ibid., loc. 218.

6. https://biblehub.com/greek/3403.htm.

7. Joanna Collicutt and Roger Bretherton, *Being Mindful, Being Christian: A Guide to Mindful Discipleship* (Monarch Books, 2016), loc. 307, Kindle.

8. "A Short History of Jewish Meditation," *Velveteen Rabbi* (blog), February 10, 2014, http://velveteenrabbi.blogs.com/blog/2014/02/jewish-meditation.html.

9. A. W. Tozer, *The Pursuit of God* (New York: Start Publishing LLC, 2013), 61.

10. Richard J. Foster, *Sanctuary of the Soul: Journey into Meditative Prayer* (Downers Grove, IL: IVP Books, 2011), loc. 106–18, Kindle.

11. Adele Ahlberg Calhoun, *Spiritual Disciplines Handbook: Practices That Transform Us* (Downers Grove, IL: IVP Books, 2009), loc. 3488, Kindle.

12. Reynolds, *Living with the Mind*, loc. 108.

13. Tom Schwanda, *Soul Recreation: The Contemplative-Mystical Piety of Puritanism* (Eugene, OR: Pickwick Publications, 2015), 17.

14. Ibid., 75

15. Kim Nataraja, *Journey to the Heart: Christian Contemplation through the Centuries—An Illustrated Guide* (Maryknoll, NY: Orbis Books, 2012), 97.

16. Calhoun, *Spiritual Disciplines Handbook*, 17–18.

17. Cynthia Bourgeault, *Centering Prayer and Inner Awakening* (Lanham, MD: Cowley Publications, 2004), loc. 702, Kindle.

18. Bernard McGinn, *The Foundations of Mysticism: Origins to the Fifth Century* (New York: The Crossroad Publishing Company, 2004), 64.

19. Shaun Lambert, "Elements of #mindfulness Emerging in Early Christian Spirituality," *The Free Running Mind* (blog), February 15, 2013, https://shaunlambert.co.uk/2013/02/15/elements-of-mindfulness-emerging-in-early-christian-spirituality.

20. Reynolds, *Living with the Mind*, loc. 1254–71.

21. Nataraja, *Journey to the Heart*, 63.

22. Aaron, "John Calvin: Knowledge of God, Knowledge of Self," October 15, 2009, http://apologeticjunkie.blogspot.com/2009/10/john-calvin-knowledge-of-god-knowledge.html.

23. Tom Schwanda, *Soul Recreation*, 41.

24. Collicutt and Bretherton, *Being Mindful, Being Christian*, loc. 887.

25. Ursula King, *Christian Mystics: Their Lives and Legacies throughout the Ages* (Mahwah, NJ: HiddenSpring, 2001), loc. 1119, Kindle.

26. *Reading the Christian Spiritual Classics: A Guide for Evangelicals,* Jamin Goggin and Kyle C. Strobel, eds. (Downers Grove, IL: IVP Academic, 2013), loc. 4150, Kindle.

27. Trevin Wax, "How D. L. Moody Paved the Way for Today's Evangelicals," *The Gospel Coalition* (blog), September 10, 2014, www.thegospelcoalition.org/blogs/trevin-wax/how-d-l-moody-paved-the-way-for-todays-evangelicals.

28. E. Lynn Harris, *The Mystic Spirituality of A. W. Tozer, a Twentieth-Century American Protestant* (San Francisco: Edwin Mellen Pr, 1992).

Chapter 3: The BREATHe Model: The Six Bible-Based Practices of Holy Noticing

1. Martin Laird, *Into the Silent Land: A Guide to the Practice of Contemplation* (London: Darton Longman and Todd, 2006), 3.

2. Susan L. Smalley and Diana Winston, *Fully Present: The Science,*

Art, and Practice of Mindfulness (Boston: Da Capo Press, 2010), loc. 390, Kindle.

3. Daniel Goleman and Richard J. Davidson, *Altered Traits: Science Reveals How Meditation Changes Your Mind, Brain, and Body* (New York: Avery, 2017), 77–78.

4. Cynthia Bourgeault, *Centering Prayer and Inner Awakening* (Lanham, MD: Cowley Publications, 2004), loc. 339, Kindle.

5. Laird, *Into the Silent Land*, 37–38.

6. G. E. H. Palmer, Philip Sherrard, and Bishop Kallistos Ware, trans., *Philokalia—The Eastern Christian Spiritual Texts: Selections Annotated and Explained* (Woodstock, VT: SkyLight Paths, 2012), loc. 2338, Kindle.

7. Kim Nataraja, *Journey to the Heart: Christian Contemplation through the Centuries—An Illustrated Guide* (Maryknoll, NY: Orbis Books, 2012), 338.

8. Thomas Keating, *Open Mind, Open Heart* (New York: Bloomsbury, 2006), 32.

9. Vbalaba, "How Much Air Do We Breathe in a Lifetime?," The Tipsters, January 5, 2013, https://thetipsters.wordpress. com/2013/01/05/how-much-air-do-we-breathe-in-a-lifetime.

10. Alex Korb, PhD, *The Upward Spiral: Using Neuroscience to Reverse the Course of Depression, One Small Change at a Time*, (Oakland, CA: New Harbinger Publications, 2015), 147–48.

11. Bessel van der Kolk, *The Body Keeps the Score: Brain, Mind, and Body in the Healing of Trauma* (New York: Penguin Books, 2014), 207.

12. Van der Kolk, *The Body Keeps the Score*, 268.

13. Matthew MacKinnon, "The Myth of Multitasking: Why Your Brain Lacks the Capital to Pay Attention to Two Things at Once," *Psychology Today*, January 5, 2016, www.psychologytoday.com/blog/ the-neuroscience-mindfulness/201601/the-myth-multitasking.

14. Kirk Warren Brown, J. David Creswell, and Richard M. Ryan, eds., *Handbook of Mindfulness: Theory, Research, and Practice* (Plymouth, UK: Guilford Press, 2015), loc. 8797, Kindle.

15. Daniel B. Levinson et al., "A Mind You Can Count On: Validating Breath Counting as a Behavioral Measure of Mindfulness," *Frontiers in Psychology* 5 (October 24, 2014), https://doi.org/10.3389/ fpsyg.2014.01202.

16. Romeo Vitelli, PhD, "Letting Your Mind Wander: What Are the Pros and Cons of Mind-Wandering?," *Psychology Today*, April 15, 2013,,www.psychologytoday.com/ca/blog/media-spotlight/201304/ letting-your-mind-wander

17. Peter R. Killeen, "Absent without Leave; a Neuroenergetic Theory of Mind Wandering," *Frontiers in Psychology* 4 (July 2013), https:// doi.org/10.3389/fpsyg.2013.00373.

18. Keating, *Open Mind*, 22.

19. Tricia McCary Rhodes, *The Wired Soul: Finding Spiritual Balance in a Hyperconnected Age* (Colorado Springs, CO: NavPress, 2016), loc. 1302–17, Kindle.

Chapter 4: Practice One: Ponder and Yield Your Body

1. Kirk D. Strosahl and Patricia J. Robinson, *In This Moment: Five Steps to Transcending Stress Using Mindfulness and Neuroscience,* (Oakland, CA: New Harbinger Publications, 2015), loc. 147, Kindle.
2. Bronwyn Fryer, "Are You Working Too Hard?," Harvard Business Review, November 2005, https://hbr.org/2005/11/are-you-working-too-hard.
3. Armita Golkar et al., "The Influence of Work-Related Chronic Stress on the Regulation of Emotion and on Functional Connectivity in the Brain," *PLOS ONE* 9, no. 9 (September 3, 2014): e104550, https://doi.org/10.1371/journal.pone.0104550.
4. Kerry J. Ressler, "Amygdala Activity, Fear, and Anxiety: Modulation by Stress," *Biological Psychiatry* 67, no. 12 (June 15, 2010): 1117–19, https://doi.org/10.1016/j.biopsych.2010.04.027.
5. Sandra Blakeslee, "A Small Part of the Brain, and Its Profound Effects," *New York Times*, February 6, 2007, www.nytimes.com/2007/02/06/health/psychology/06brain.html.
6. This is called interoception. Hideyuki Takahashi et al., "The Anterior Insula Tracks Behavioral Entropy during an Interpersonal Competitive Game," *PLoS ONE* 10, no. 6 (June 3, 2015), https://doi.org/10.1371/journal.pone.0123329.
7. Roy F. Baumeister et al., "Bad Is Stronger than Good," *Review of General Psychology* 5, no. 4 (2001): 323–70, https://doi.org/10.1037/1089-2680.5.4.323.
8. This part of the brain is called the prefrontal cortex.
9. "In Control of Your Life? 3 Techniques for Managing Your Inner Chimp," *Brilliant Living HQ* (blog), accessed December 21, 2017, www.brilliantlivinghq.com/in-control-of-your-life-3-techniques-for-managing-your-inner-chimp.
10. The process of turning short-term memory into long-term memory is called consolidation.
11. The brain's emotional accelerator is called the sympathetic nervous system.
12. The brain's emotional brake is called the parasympathetic nervous system.
13. This system is called the HPA axis, an acronym for three brain parts that work together in the stress response—the hypothalamus, the pituitary gland, and the adrenal glands.
14. This calm hormonal and emotional balance is called homeostasis.
15. Karen O'Leary, Siobhan O'Neill, and Samantha Dockray, "A Systematic Review of the Effects of Mindfulness Interventions on

Cortisol," *Journal of Health Psychology* 21, no. 9 (September 2016): 2108–21, https://doi.org/10.1177/1359105315569095.

16. Scott Barry Kaufman and Carolyn Gregoire, *Wired to Create: Unraveling the Mysteries of the Creative Mind* (New York: TarcherPerigee, 2015), 112–13.

17. Daniel Goleman and Richard J. Davidson, *Altered Traits: Science Reveals How Meditation Changes Your Mind, Brain, and Body* (New York: Avery, 2017), 179.

18. Andrew J. Howell, Nancy L. Digdon, and Karen Buro, "Mindfulness Predicts Sleep-Related Self-Regulation and Well-Being," *Personality and Individual Differences* 48, no. 4 (March 2010): 419–24, https://doi.org/10.1016/j.paid.2009.11.009.

19. Shiloh Rea, "Neurobiological Changes Explain How Mindfulness Meditation Improves Health," Carnegie Mellon University, February 4, 2016, www.cmu.edu/news/stories/archives/2016/february/meditation-changes-brain.html.

20. Ivana Buric et al., "What Is the Molecular Signature of Mind–Body Interventions? A Systematic Review of Gene Expression Changes Induced by Meditation and Related Practices," *Frontiers in Immunology* 8 (2017), https://doi.org/10.3389/fimmu.2017.00670.

21. Annette M. Mankus et al., "Mindfulness and Heart Rate Variability in Individuals with High and Low Generalized Anxiety Symptoms," *Behaviour Research and Therapy* 51, no. 7 (July 2013): 386–91, https://doi.org/10.1016/j.brat.2013.03.005.

22. Elizabeth A. Hoge et al., "Loving-Kindness Meditation Practice Associated with Longer Telomeres in Women," *Brain, Behavior, and Immunity* 32 (August 2013): 159–63, https://doi.org/10.1016/j.bbi.2013.04.005.

23. Marlynn Wei, "You Can Practice Mindfulness in as Little as 15 Minutes a Day," Harvard Health Publishing, November 2015, www.health.harvard.edu/mind-and-mood/you-can-practice-mindfulness-in-as-little-as-15-minutes-a-day.

24. Dana Fischer, Matthias Messner, and Olga Pollatos, "Improvement of Interoceptive Processes after an 8-Week Body Scan Intervention," *Frontiers in Human Neuroscience* 11 (September 12, 2017), https://doi.org/10.3389/fnhum.2017.00452.

25. Mark R. McMinn, *The Science of Virtue: Why Positive Psychology Matters to the Church* (Ada, MI: Brazos Press, 2017), 78.

26. *Greater Good* magazine, "Study Shows How Practicing Gratitude Can Help Train Your Brain and Improve Mental Health over Time," *SharpBrains* (blog), July 5, 2017, https://sharpbrains.com/blog/2017/07/05/study-shows-how-practicing-gratitude-can-help-train-your-brain-and-improve-mental-health-over-time.

27. Joanna Collicutt and Roger Bretherton, *Being Mindful, Being Christian: A Guide to Mindful Discipleship* (Monarch Books, 2016), 187.

28. Ibid., 189.

29. This process is called mentalizing.

Chapter 5: Practice Two: Review and Renew Your Relationships

1. W. Oscar Thompson Jr. and Carolyn Ritzman, *Concentric Circles of Concern: Seven Stages for Making Disciples*, ed. Claude V. King (Nashville: B&H Publishing Group, 1999).

2. Julianne McGill, Francesca Adler-Baeder, Priscilla Rodriguez, "Mindfully in Love: A Meta-Analysis of the Association between Mindfulness and Relationship Satisfaction," *Journal of Human Sciences and Extension* 4, no.1, (2016), https://docs.wixstatic.com/ugd/c8fe6e_65448e5da9754a6c8676f179d07067d1.pdf.

3. This part of the brain is called the default mode network, the network that activates when we are not actively attending to a task. It involves parts of our brain from the center portion behind our forehead all the way back to the back part of our brain in a swath like a Mohawk haircut.

4. Kathleen A. Garrison et al., "Meditation Leads to Reduced Default Mode Network Activity beyond an Active Task," *Cognitive, Affective & Behavioral Neuroscience* 15, no. 3 (September 2015): 712–20, https://doi.org/10.3758/s13415-015-0358-3.

5. Tricia McCary Rhodes, *The Wired Soul: Finding Spiritual Balance in a Hyperconnected Age* (Colorado Springs, CO: NavPress, 2016), loc. 1722–24, Kindle.

6. Charles Stone, *Brain-Savvy Leaders: The Science of Significant Ministry* (Nashville: Abingdon Press, 2015), loc. 2322–36, Kindle.

7. Mirror neurons, the insula, and the prefrontal cortex compose the hub of this resonance circuit. Mindfulness increases insula activity. See, Sara W. Lazar et al., "Meditation Experience Is Associated with Increased Cortical Thickness," *Neuroreport* 16, no. 17 (November 28, 2005): 1893–97, www.ncbi.nlm.nih.gov/pmc/articles/PMC1361002.

8. Kirk Warren Brown, J. David Creswell, and Richard M. Ryan, eds., *Handbook of Mindfulness: Theory, Research, and Practice* (Plymouth, UK: Guilford Press, 2015), loc. 5995.

9. Jennifer S. Mascaro et al., "The Neural Mediators of Kindness-Based Meditation: A Theoretical Model," *Frontiers inn Psychology* 6 (2015), www.ncbi.nlm.nih.gov/pmc/articles/PMC4325657.

10. Brown, Creswell, and Ryan, *Handbook of Mindfulness*, loc. 6005.

11. The technical word for reading between the lines is *mentalizing*, the ability to intuit the thoughts, feelings, and intentions of others as we attend to our own mental states. The process is called *Theory of Mind*. That is, I have a theory of what is going on inside your mind. It is not mind reading but more like the spiritual gift of discernment, and it's based in neuroscience. The process is mostly experienced in

day-to-day interaction with others. Mirror neurons are apparently involved in this ability.

12. Brown, Creswell, and Ryan, *Handbook of Mindfulness,* 42ff.

13. Jennifer S. Mascaro et al., "Compassion Meditation Enhances Empathic Accuracy and Related Neural Activity," *Social Cognitive and Affective Neuroscience* 8, no. 1 (January 1, 2013): 48–55, https://doi.org/10.1093/scan/nss095.

14. Antoine Lutz et al., "Long-Term Meditators Self-Induce High-Amplitude Gamma Synchrony during Mental Practice," *Proceedings of the National Academy of Sciences* 101, no. 46 (November 16, 2004): 16369–73, https://doi.org/10.1073/pnas.0407401101.

15. Helen Y. Weng et al., "Compassion Training Alters Altruism and Neural Responses to Suffering," *Psychological Science* 24, no. 7 (July 1, 2013): 1171–80, https://doi.org/10.1177/0956797612469537.

16. Called "trait" mindfulness.

17. Brown, Creswell, and Ryan, *Handbook of Mindfulness*, loc. 5773.

18. Daniel Goleman and Richard J. Davidson, *Altered Traits: Science Reveals How Meditation Changes Your Mind, Brain, and Body* (New York: Avery, 2017), 113.

19. These chemicals are called neurotransmitters, and empathy causes oxytocin to surge as well as instigating the release of dopamine and serotonin.

20. Paul J. Zak, *The Moral Molecule: How Trust Works* (New York: Plume, 2012), loc. 995, Kindle.

21. Brent J. Atkinson, "Mindfulness Training and the Cultivation of Secure, Satisfying Couple Relationships," *Couple and Family Psychology: Research and Practice* 2, no. 2 (2013): 73–94, https://doi.org/10.1037/cfp0000002.

22. Brown, Creswell, and Ryan, *Handbook of Mindfulness,* loc. 6114.

23. Goleman and Davidson, *Altered Traits*, loc. 1485.

24. Jennifer Block-Lerner et al., "The Case for Mindfulness-Based Approaches in the Cultivation of Empathy: Does Nonjudgmental, Present-Moment Awareness Increase Capacity for Perspective-Taking and Empathic Concern?," *Journal of Marital and Family Therapy* 33, no. 4 (October 2007): 501–16, https://doi.org/10.1111/j.1752-0606.2007.00034.x.

25. Sean Barnes et al., "The Role of Mindfulness in Romantic Relationship Satisfaction and Responses to Relationship Stress," *Journal of Marital and Family Therapy* 33, no. 4 (October 2007): 482–500, https://doi.org/10.1111/j.1752-0606.2007.00033.x.

26. Brown, Creswell, and Ryan, *Handbook of Mindfulness*, loc. 3061.

27. Daniel J. Siegel, *Mindsight: The New Science of Personal Transformation* (New York: Bantam, 2010), loc. 1111ff, Kindle.

28. Matt Tenney and Tim Gard, *The Mindfulness Edge: How to Rewire Your Brain for Leadership and Personal Excellence without Adding to Your Schedule* (Hoboken, NJ: Wiley, 2016), loc. 3610–22, Kindle.

Chapter 6: Practice Three: Notice and Engage Your Environment

1. Linda Stone, quoted in David Rock, *Your Brain at Work: Strategies for Overcoming Distraction, Regaining Focus, and Working Smarter All Day Long* (New York: HarperCollins, 2009), 36.

2. Tony Reinke, *12 Ways Your Phone Is Changing You* (Wheaton, IL: Crossway, 2017), loc. 200, Kindle.

3. Adam Gazzaley and Larry D. Rosen, *The Distracted Mind: Ancient Brains in a High-Tech World* (Cambridge, MA: The MIT Press, 2016), 109.

4. Larry D. Rosen, "We Didn't Start the Fire: Why Kids Consume Massive Amounts of Media and Multitask All Day (and Night) Long," *Psychology Today*, May 3, 2010, www.psychologytoday.com/blog/rewired-the-psychology-technology/201005/we-didnt-start-the-fire-why-kids-consume-massive.

5. Kevin McSpadden, "You Now Have a Shorter Attention Span Than a Goldfish," *Time*, May 14, 2015, http://time.com/3858309/attention-spans-goldfish.

6. Manoush Zomorodi, *Bored and Brilliant: How Spacing Out Can Unlock Your Most Productive and Creative Self* (New York: St. Martin's Press, 2017), loc. 1551, Kindle.

7. Tim Keller (@ timkellernyc), Twitter, @RyanWortman: "Why do you think young Christian adults struggle most deeply with God as a personal reality in their lives." December 31, 2013, https://twitter.com/timkellernyc/status/418124221101772800.

8. Reinke, *12 Ways*, loc. 771.

9. Ibid., loc. 716ff.

10. Margaret Emory, "The Divided Brain: An Interview with Dr. Iain McGilchrist," *Brain World*, March 7, 2018, http://brainworldmagazine.com/what-at-any-one-moment-is-governing-our-actions.

11. Authors Fabritius and Hagemann explain that three brain chemicals interplay in attention, norepenphrine (alerting function), dopamine (attending function), and acetylcholine (sustaining function). Friederike Fabritius and Hans W. Hagemann, *The Leading Brain: Powerful Science-Based Strategies for Achieving Peak Performance* (New York: TarcherPerigee, 2017), loc. 246, Kindle.

12. Attention involves two components that compete against each other: focus (selecting what we pay attention to) and ignore (blocking out irrelevant information). So, to pay attention, we must selectively attend to something and suppress other information. What our goals are directs where we pay attention. Let's say you want to buy your son a puppy. Your goal, buy a puppy, will help you focus on the puppies at the pet store while ignoring the kittens. Three limitations affect how well we pay attention—the speed at which we pay attention (how fast we can switch our attention from one thing to the next), how long we can sustain our attention (called

attention span), and how well we can distribute our attention (think of a fisherman casting a net).

13. Daniel Goldman, "Meditation: A Practical Way to Retrain Attention," Mindful, November 20, 2013, www.mindful.org/meditation-a-practical-way-to-retrain-attention.

14. Jeffrey Schwartz and Rebecca Gladding, *You Are Not Your Brain: The 4-Step Solution for Changing Bad Habits, Ending Unhealthy Thinking, and Taking Control of Your Life* (New York: Avery, 2011), loc. 1022–27, Kindle.

15. Michael Chaskalson, *Mindfulness in Eight Weeks: The Revolutionary 8 Week Plan to Clear Your Mind and Calm Your Life* (London: HarperThorsons, 2014), loc. 988ff, Kindle.

16. Drew Dyck, *Your Future Self Will Thank You: Secrets to Self-Control from the Bible and Brain Science* (Chicago: Moody Publishers, 2019), 113.

17. Two process are at work in missing what is right under our noses: inattentional blindness (blind to what is really happening) and a similar one called attentional blink—when we've used up our attentional resources on one thing that causes our attention to blink, which makes us miss the next thing.

18. Lorenza S. Colzato et al., "Meditation-Induced States Predict Attentional Control over Time," *Consciousness and Cognition* 37 (December 2015): 57–62, https://doi.org/10.1016/j.concog.2015.08.006.

19. Michael D. Mrazek et al., "Mindfulness Training Improves Working Memory Capacity and GRE Performance While Reducing Mind Wandering," *Psychological Science* 24, no. 5 (May 2013): 776–81, https://doi.org/10.1177/0956797612459659.

20. "Mindful Multitasking: Meditation First Can Calm Stress, Aid Concentration," ScienceDaily, June 14, 2012, www.sciencedaily.com/releases/2012/06/120614094118.htm.

21. Martin Laird, *A Sunlit Absence: Silence, Awareness, and Contemplation.* (New York: Oxford University Press, 2011), loc. 232–33, Kindle.

22. Daniel J. Simons and Daniel T. Levin, "Failure to Detect Change to People during a Real-World Interaction," *ResearchGate* 5, no. 4 (December 1, 1998): 644–49, https://doi.org/10.3758/BF03208840.

23. Lisa A. Kilpatrick et al., "Impact of Mindfulness-Based Stress Reduction Training on Intrinsic Brain Connectivity," *NeuroImage* 56, no. 1 (May 1, 2011): 290–98, https://doi.org/10.1016/j.neuroimage.2011.02.034.

24. Heleen A. Slagter, Richard J. Davidson, and Antoine Lutz, "Mental Training as a Tool in the Neuroscientific Study of Brain and Cognitive Plasticity," *Frontiers in Human Neuroscience* 5 (2011): 17, https://doi.org/10.3389/fnhum.2011.00017.

25. Ray Rhodes, *Susie* (Chicago: Moody Publishers, 2018), 190; quote within quote: C. H. Spurgeon, *C.H. Spurgeon's Autobiography:*

Compiled from His Diary, Letters, and Records, by His Wife, and His Private Secretary (London: Passmore and Alabaster, 1897–99; repr., Pasadena, TX: Pilgrim Publications, 1992), 2:293.

Chapter 7: Practice Four: Label and Release Your Afflictive Emotions (Affect)

1. Dr. Jeremy Dean, "Why Thought-Suppression Is Counter-Productive," *Pysblog* (blog), May 22, 2009, www.spring.org.uk/2009/05/why-thought-suppression-is-counter-productive.php.
2. "The Four Components of Emotion Definition," ResearchGate, accessed July 20, 2018, www.researchgate.net/figure/The-four-components-of-emotion-definition-Source-after-Reeve-2009_fig2_269631983.
3. Steven C. Hayes with Spencer Smith, *Get Out of Your Mind and Into Your Life: The New Acceptance and Commitment Therapy* (Oakland, CA: New Harbinger Publications, 2005), loc. 810, Kindle.
4. Timothy Keller, *God's Wisdom for Navigating Life: A Year of Daily Devotions in the Book of Proverbs* (New York: Viking, 2017), loc. 2123, Kindle.
5. Kirk A. Bingaman, *The Power of Neuroplasticity for Pastoral and Spiritual Care* (Lanham, MD: Lexington Books, 2014), loc. 1257–62, Kindle.
6. This is called our default mode. See Jason Castro, "A Wandering Mind Is an Unhappy One: New Research Indicates the Wisdom of Being Absorbed in What You Do," Scientific American, November 24, 2010, www.scientificamerican.com/article.cfm?id=a-wandering-mind-is-an-un.
7. Bryan Lowe, "The Depression Epidemic," *Broken Believers* (blog), March 2, 2016, https://brokenbelievers.com/2016/03/02/the-depression-epidemic.
8. Catherine M. Pittman and Elizabeth M. Karle, *Rewire Your Anxious Brain: How to Use the Neuroscience of Fear to End Anxiety, Panic, and Worry* (Oakland, CA: New Harbinger Publications, 2015), loc. 263, Kindle.
9. "C. S. Lewis Quotes: Daily Wisdom from the Writings of C. S. Lewis," September 14, 2011, Tumblr, http://cslewisquotes.tumblr.com/post/10207082251/god-could-had-he-pleased-have-been-incarnate-in.
10. Kirk Warren Brown, J. David Creswell, and Richard M. Ryan, eds., *Handbook of Mindfulness: Theory, Research, and Practice* (The Guilford Press, 2015), 42ff.
11. Bingaman, *The Power of Neuroplasticity,* loc. 240.
12. Ibid., loc. 85–87.
13. Ashley Borders, Mitch Earleywine, and Archana Jajodia, "Could Mindfulness Decrease Anger, Hostility, and Aggression by Decreasing Rumination?," *Aggressive Behavior* 36, no. 1 (January 1, 2010):

28–44, https://doi.org/10.1002/ab.20327.

14. Daniel J. Siegel, *Mindsight: The New Science of Personal Transformation* (New York: Bantam, 2010), loc. 2360, Kindle.

15. Richard J. Davidson and Sharon Begley, *The Emotional Life of Your Brain: How Its Unique Patterns Affect the Way You Think, Feel, and Live—and How You Can Change Them* (New York: Hudson Street Press, 2012), loc. 4481, Kindle.

16. "Daily Meditation Practice Key to Positive Emotions," American Mindfulness Research Association, September 19, 2017, https://goamra.org/daily-meditation-practice-key-positive-emotions.

17. Ed Diener, Richard E. Lucas, and Christie Napa Scollon, "Beyond the Hedonic Treadmill: Revising the Adaptation Theory of Well-Being," *American Psychologist* 61, no. 4 (2006): 305–14, https://doi.org/10.1037/0003-066X.61.4.305.

18. Ibid.

19. Amber S. Emanuel et al., "The Role of Mindfulness Facets in Affective Forecasting," *Personality and Individual Differences* 49, no. 7 (November 1, 2010): 815–18, https://doi.org/10.1016/j.paid.2010.06.012.

20. This is called affective forecasting.

21. Brown, Creswell, and Ryan, *Handbook of Mindfulness*, loc. 4652.

22. Baljinder K. Sahdra et al., "Enhanced Response Inhibition during Intensive Meditation Training Predicts Improvements in Self-Reported Adaptive Socioemotional Functioning," *Emotion (Washington, D.C.)* 11, no. 2 (April 2011): 299–312, https://doi.org/10.1037/a0022764.

23. Brown, Creswell, and Ryan, *Handbook of Mindfulness*, loc. 5351.

24. Susan L. Smalley and Diana Winston, *Fully Present: The Science, Art, and Practice of Mindfulness* (Boston: Da Capo Press, 2010), loc. 145, Kindle.

25. Brown, Creswell, and Ryan, *Handbook of Mindfulness*, loc. 3625,.

26. Travis Bradberry and Jean Greaves, *Emotional Intelligence 2.0* (San Diego:TalentSmart, 2009), loc. 339, Kindle.

27. Paul A. Frewen et al., "Clinical and Neural Correlates of Alexithymia in Posttraumatic Stress Disorder," *Journal of Abnormal Psychology* 117, no. 1 (February 2008): 171–81, https://doi.org/10.1037/0021-843X.117.1.171.

28. Matthew D. Lieberman, *Social: Why Our Brains Are Wired to Connect* (Crown, 2013), loc. 3123, Kindle.

29. This is called valence.

30. This is called arousal.

31. This diagram is called a circumplex. See Jonathan Posner, James A. Russell, and Bradley S. Peterson, "The Circumplex Model of Affect: An Integrative Approach to Affective Neuroscience, Cognitive Development, and Psychopathology," *Development and*

Psychopathology 17, no. 3 (2005): 715–34, https://doi.org/10.1017/
S0954579405050340.

32. Pittman and Karle, *Rewire Your Anxious Brain*, chapter 9.
33. Brown, Creswell, and Ryan, *Handbook of Mindfulness*, loc. 5444.

Chapter 8: Practice Five: Observe and Submit Your Thoughts

1. Oswald Chambers, *My Utmost for His Highest*, rev. ed., ed. James
   Reimann (Grand Rapids, MI: Discovery House Publishers, 2010),
   loc. 4225, Kindle
2. Martin Laird, *Into the Silent Land: A Guide to the Practice of
   Contemplation* (London: Darton Longman and Todd, 2006), 19–20.
3. Susan David, *Emotional Agility: Get Unstuck, Embrace Change, and
   Thrive in Work and Life* (New York: Avery, 2016), loc. 311, Kindle.
4. Jonathan Haidt, *The Happiness Hypothesis: Finding Modern Truth
   in Ancient Wisdom* (New York: Basic Books, 2006), 30–31.
5. Siobhan Kelleher Kukolic, "The average person has between 12,000
   and 60,000 thoughts per day," Siobhankukolic.com, June 11, 2018,
   https://siobhankukolic.com/the-average-person-has-between-
   12000-and-60000-thoughts-per-day/.
6. William R Marchand, "Neural Mechanisms of Mindfulness and
   Meditation: Evidence from Neuroimaging Studies," *World Journal of
   Radiology* 6, no. 7 (July 28, 2014): 471–79, https://doi.org/10.4329/
   wjr.v6.i7.471.
7. Stefan Gillow Reynolds, *Living with the Mind of Christ: Mindfulness in Christian Spirituality* (London: Darton, Longman and Todd
   Ltd, 2016), loc. 1458, Kindle.
8. Tim Stead, *Mindfulness and Christian Spirituality: Making Space
   for God* (London, UK: SPCK, 2016), loc. 1340, Kindle.
9. Yoona Kang, June Gruber, and Jeremy R. Gray, "Mindfulness
   and De-Automatization," *Emotion Review* 5, no. 2 (April 1, 2013):
   192–201, https://doi.org/10.1177/1754073912451629.
10. Overly identifying with our thoughts is called *cognitive fusion*,
    a term used in a type of therapy called ACT (Acceptance and
    Commitment Therapy), a therapy shown to be effective in treating
    depression, anxiety, and chronic pain.
11. Steven C. Hayes with Spencer Smith, *Get Out of Your Mind and
    Into Your Life: The New Acceptance and Commitment Therapy*
    (Oakland, CA: New Harbinger Publications, 2005), loc. 1596, Kindle.
12. This is a process called de-fusion, when we mentally disconnect
    ourselves from unhealthy thoughts and emotions.
13. Bob Stahl and Elisha Goldstein, *A Mindfulness-Based Stress Reduc-
    tion Workbook*, Pap/MP3 Wk edition (New Harbinger Publications,
    2010), loc. 1173, Kindle.
14. Melanie Greenberg, PhD, *The Stress-Proof Brain: Master Your
    Emotional Response to Stress Using Mindfulness and Neuroplasticity*
    (Oakland, CA: New Harbinger Publications, 2017). loc. 2377, Kindle.

15. Curt Thompson, MD, *Anatomy of the Soul: Surprising Connections between Neuroscience and Spiritual Practices That Can Transform Your Life and Relationships* (Carol Stream, IL: Tyndale Momentum, 2010), loc. 3996, Kindle.

16. Amishi P. Jha et al., "Examining the Protective Effects of Mindfulness Training on Working Memory Capacity and Affective Experience," *Emotion (Washington, D.C.)* 10, no. 1 (February 2010): 54–64, https://doi.org/10.1037/a0018438.

17. B. Johansson, H. Bjuhr, and L. Rönnbäck, "Mindfulness-Based Stress Reduction (MBSR) Improves Long-Term Mental Fatigue after Stroke or Traumatic Brain Injury," *Brain Injury* 26, no. 13–14 (July 13, 2012): 1621–28, https://doi.org/10.3109/02699052.2012.700082.

18. Adam Moore and Peter Malinowski, "Meditation, Mindfulness and Cognitive Flexibility," *Consciousness and Cognition* 18, no. 1 (March 2009): 176–86, https://doi.org/10.1016/j.concog.2008.12.008.

19. Xiaoqian Ding et al., "Improving Creativity Performance by Short-Term Meditation," *Behavioral and Brain Functions: BBF* 10 (March 2014): 9, https://doi.org/10.1186/1744-9081-10-9.

20. Laird, *Into the Silent Land*, loc. 263, Kindle.

21. Catherine M. Pittman and Elizabeth M. Karle, *Rewire Your Anxious Brain: How to Use the Neuroscience of Fear to End Anxiety, Panic, and Worry* (Oakland, CA: New Harbinger Publications, 2015), loc. 2553, Kindle.,

22. Mark Williams and Danny Penman, Mindfulness: An Eight-Week Plan for Finding Peace in a Frantic World (New York: Rodale, 2012), loc. 226, Kindle.

23. Timothy D. Wilson et al., "Just Think: The Challenges of the Disengaged Mind," *Science* 345, no. 6192 (July 4, 2014): 75–77, https://doi.org/10.1126/science.1250830.

24. Andrew Bonar, *Memoir and Remains of the Rev. Robert Murray McCheyne* (Edinburgh: William Oliphant and Co., 1864), 293.

25. Dilwar Hussain, "Meta-Cognition in Mindfulness: A Conceptual Analysis," *Psychological Thought* 8, no. 2 (October 16, 2015): 132–41.

Chapter 9: Practice Six: Search and Surrender Your Heart

1. John M. Darley and C. Daniel Batson, "'From Jerusalem to Jericho': A Study of Situational and Dispositional Variables in Helping Behavior," *Journal of Personality and Social Psychology* 27, no. 1 (1973): 100–108, https://doi.org/10.1037/h0034449.

2. Timothy Keller, *God's Wisdom for Navigating Life: A Year of Daily Devotions in the Book of Proverbs*, (New York: Viking, 2017), loc. 1809, Kindle.

3. Ryan M. Niemiec, *Mindfulness and Character Strengths A Practical Guide to Flourishing* (Boston: Hogrefe Publishing, 2013).

4. Kelly McGonigal, PhD, "How Mindfulness Makes the Brain

Immune to Temptation: Paying Attention to Cravings Takes Away Their Power," *Psychology Today*, November 27, 2011, www. psychologytoday.com/blog/the-science-willpower/201111/ how-mindfulness-makes-the-brain-immune-temptation.

5. Esther K. Papies, Lawrence W. Barsalou, and Ruud Custers, "Mindful Attention Prevents Mindless Impulses," *Social Psychological and Personality Science* 3, no. 3 (May 1, 2012): 291–99, https://doi.org/10.1177/1948550611419031.

6. Shauna L. Shapiro, Hooria Jazaieri, and Philippe R. Goldin, "Mindfulness-Based Stress Reduction Effects on Moral Reasoning and Decision Making," *The Journal of Positive Psychology* 7, no. 6 (September 11, 2012): 504–15, https://doi.org/10.1080/17439760.2012.723732.

7. Shaun Lambert, *Putting on the Wakeful One: Attuning to the Spirit of Jesus through Watchfulness* (Watford, UK: Instant Apostle, 2016), loc. 1427, Kindle.

8. J. P. Moreland, *Love Your God with All Your Mind: The Role of Reason in the Life of the Soul*, rev. ed. (Colorado Springs, CO: NavPress, 2012), 73.

9. Ibid., 75.

10. This is an interesting paper from secular research on the effects of mindfulness on character development. Ryan Niemiec, Tayyab Rashid, and Marcello Spinella, "Strong Mindfulness: Integrating Mindfulness and Character Strengths," *Journal of Mental Health Counseling* 34, no. 3 (July 2012): 240–53, https://doi.org/10.17744/mehc.34.3.34p6328x2v204v21.

11. Rob Moll, *What Your Body Knows about God: How We Are Designed to Connect, Serve and Thrive* (Downers Grove, IL: IVP Books, 2014), 23–27.

12. Kirk A. Bingaman, *The Power of Neuroplasticity for Pastoral and Spiritual Care* (Lanham, MD: Lexington Books, 2014), loc. 1261, Kindle.

13. Brianna S. Schuyler et al., "Temporal Dynamics of Emotional Responding: Amygdala Recovery Predicts Emotional Traits," *Social Cognitive and Affective Neuroscience* 9, no. 2 (February 2014): 176–81, https://doi.org/10.1093/scan/nss131.

14. Kristin D. Neff, Ya-Ping Hsieh, and Kullaya Dejitterat, "Self-Compassion, Achievement Goals, and Coping with Academic Failure," *Self and Identity* 4, no. 3 (2005): 263–87, https://doi.org/10.1080/13576500444000317.

15. Claire E. Adams and Mark R. Leary, "Promoting Self–Compassionate Attitudes toward Eating among Restrictive and Guilty Eaters," *Journal of Social and Clinical Psychology* 26, no. 10 (December 1, 2007): 1120–44, https://doi.org/10.1521/jscp.2007.26.10.1120.

16. Kristin D. Neff, "The Role of Self-Compassion in Development: A

Healthier Way to Relate to Oneself," *Human Development* 52, no. 4 (June 2009): 211–14, https://doi.org/10.1159/000215071.

17. This is called metacognition.

18. This is called interoception.

19. This is called mentalizing. As author Valerie Porr notes, "It's the ability to step into another person's mind, while stepping outside your own." It's like having a dual lens on interpersonal interactions. It enables us to pause and think about why this person is responding as they are, while at the same time considering your motivations. www.freedominstitute.org/what-is-mentalizing.

20. This is called proprioception.

21. Oswald Chambers, *My Utmost for His Highest*, rev. ed., ed. James Reimann (Grand Rapids, MI: Discovery House Publishers, 2010), loc. 4043, Kindle.

22. Lee-Fan Tan et al., "Effect of Mindfulness Meditation on Brain–Computer Interface Performance," *Consciousness and Cognition* 23 (January 2014): 12–21, https://doi.org/10.1016/j.concog.2013.10.010.

23. Sara H. Konrath, Edward H. O'Brien, and Courtney Hsing, "Changes in Dispositional Empathy in American College Students over Time: A Meta-Analysis," *Personality and Social Psychology Review* 15, no. 2 (May 2011): 180–98, https://doi.org/10.1177/1088868310377395.

24. Richard J. Davidson and Sharon Begley, *The Emotional Life of Your Brain: How Its Unique Patterns Affect the Way You Think, Feel, and Live—and How You Can Change Them* (New York: Hudson Street Press, 2012), loc. 4060, Kindle.

25. David DeSteno, "The Kindness Cure," *The Atlantic*, July 21, 2015, www.theatlantic.com/health/archive/2015/07/mindfulness-meditation-empathy-compassion/398867.

26. Paul Condon, "Cultivating Compassion: The Effects of Compassion- and Mindfulness-Based Meditation on pro-Social Mental States and Behavior," *Psychology Dissertations*, August 7, 2014, http://iris.lib.neu.edu/psych_diss/35

27. Daniel Goleman and Richard J. Davidson, *Altered Traits: Science Reveals How Meditation Changes Your Mind, Brain, and Body* (New York: Avery, 2017), loc. 1457, Kindle.

28. Paul J. Zak, *The Moral Molecule: How Trust Works* (New York: Plume, 2012), loc. 1008, Kindle.

29. Doug Oman et al., "Meditation Lowers Stress and Supports Forgiveness among College Students: A Randomized Controlled Trial," *Journal of American College Health: J of ACH* 56, no. 5 (April 2008): 569–78, https://doi.org/10.3200/JACH.56.5.569-578.

30. Varun Sharma et al., "Bibliotherapy to Decrease Stress and Anxiety and Increase Resilience and Mindfulness: A Pilot Trial," *Explore (New York, NY)* 10, no. 4 (July-August 2014): 248–52, https://doi.org/10.1016/j.explore.2014.04.002.

31. Xinghua Liu et al., "Can Inner Peace Be Improved by Mindful-
ness Training: A Randomized Controlled Trial," *Stress and Health:
Journal of the International Society for the Investigation of Stress*,
November 22, 2013, https://doi.org/10.1002/smi.2551.
32. Adam Lueke and Bryan Gibson, "Mindfulness Meditation Reduces
Implicit Age and Race Bias: The Role of Reduced Automaticity of
Responding," *Social Psychological and Personality Science*, Novem-
ber 24, 2014, https://doi.org/10.1177/1948550614559651.

Conclusion: Engage the World like Christ

1. Sally Welch, *How to Be a Mindful Christian: 40 Simple Spiritual
Practices* (Norwich, UK: Canterbury Press, 2016), loc. 1608, Kindle.
2. Phillippa Lally et al., "How Are Habits Formed: Modelling Habit
Formation in the Real World," *European Journal of Social Psychology* 40, no. 6 (October 1, 2010): 998–1009, https://doi.org/10.1002/
ejsp.674.
3. "Why It's Hard to Change Unhealthy Behavior—and Why You
Should Keep Trying," Harvard Health Publishing: Harvard
Women's Health Watch, January 2007, www.health.harvard.edu/
staying-healthy/why-its-hard-to-change-unhealthy-behavior.
4. Joan Chittister, *Wisdom Distilled from the Daily: Living the Rule of
St. Benedict Today* (New York: HarperOne, 2013), loc. 2367, Kindle.
5. Bob Stahl and Elisha Goldstein, *A Mindfulness-Based Stress
Reduction Workbook* (New Harbinger Publications, 2010), loc. 1279,
Kindle.
6. Daniel Goleman and Richard J. Davidson, *Altered Traits: Science
Reveals How Meditation Changes Your Mind, Brain, and Body* (New
York: Avery, 2017), loc. 3220, Kindle.
7. J. David Creswell et al., "Brief Mindfulness Meditation Training
Alters Psychological and Neuroendocrine Responses to Social
Evaluative Stress," *Psychoneuroendocrinology* 44 (June 2014): 1–12,
https://doi.org/10.1016/j.psyneuen.2014.02.007.

Appendix A: A Full BREATHe Session

1. Dilwar Hussain, "Meta-Cognition in Mindfulness: A Conceptual
Analysis," *Psychological Thought* 8, no. 2 (October 16, 2015).

Appendix B: How Holy Noticing Affects Your Brain

1. Matthew S. Stanford, *Grace for the Afflicted: A Clinical and Biblical
Perspective on Mental Illness*, rev. ed. (IVP Books, 2017), loc. 574,
Kindle.
2. John Polkinghorne, "The Science and Religion Debate—an Introduction," The Faraday Papers, Faraday Institute for Science and Religion, April 2007, https://faraday-institute.org/resources/Faraday%20
Papers/Faraday%20Paper%201%20Polkinghorne_EN.pdf.*t Ministry*

(Nashville: Abingdon Press, 2015), loc. 139, Kindle.

3. Kirk A. Bingaman, *The Power of Neuroplasticity for Pastoral and Spiritual Care* (Lanham, MD: Lexington Books, 2014), loc. 301ff, Kindle.

4. Hundreds of scientists from various scientific fields have signed the Manifesto for a Post-Materialist Science, a document that challenges the "materialist-only" view of reality. Mario Beauregard et al., "Manifesto for a Post-Materialist Science," *Explore: The Journal of Science and Healing* 10, no. 5 (September 1, 2014): 272–74, https://doi.org/10.1016/j.explore.2014.06.008 .

5. Lorenza S. Colzato, Ayca Ozturk, and Bernhard Hommel, "Meditate to Create: The Impact of Focused-Attention and Open-Monitoring Training on Convergent and Divergent Thinking," *Frontiers in Psychology* 3 (April 18, 2012), https://doi.org/10.3389/fpsyg.2012.00116.

6. Jeffrey Schwartz and Rebecca Gladding, *You Are Not Your Brain: The 4-Step Solution for Changing Bad Habits, Ending Unhealthy Thinking, and Taking Control of Your Life* (New York: Avery, 2011), loc. 1142, Kindle.

7. Norman A. S. Farb et al., "Attending to the Present: Mindfulness Meditation Reveals Distinct Neural Modes of Self-Reference," *Social Cognitive and Affective Neuroscience* 2, no. 4 (December 1, 2007): 313–22, https://doi.org/10.1093/scan/nsm030.

8. Katherine S. Young et al., "The Impact of Mindfulness-Based Interventions on Brain Activity: A Systematic Review of Functional Magnetic Resonance Imaging Studies," *Neuroscience and Biobehavioral Reviews* 84 (January 2018): 424–33, https://doi.org/10.1016/j.neubiorev.2017.08.003.

9. Aviva Berkovich-Ohana, Joseph Glicksohn, and Abraham Goldstein, "Mindfulness-Induced Changes in Gamma Band Activity—Implications for the Default Mode Network, Self-Reference and Attention," *Clinical Neurophysiology: Official Journal of the International Federation of Clinical Neurophysiology* 123, no. 4 (April 2012): 700–710, https://doi.org/10.1016/j.clinph.2011.07.048.

10. Judson A. Brewer and Kathleen A. Garrison, "The Posterior Cingulate Cortex as a Plausible Mechanistic Target of Meditation: Findings from Neuroimaging," *Annals of the New York Academy of Sciences* 1307 (January 2014): 19–27, https://doi.org/10.1111/nyas.12246.

11. Tricia McCary Rhodes, *The Wired Soul: Finding Spiritual Balance in a Hyperconnected Age* (Colorado Springs, CO: NavPress, 2016), loc. 1191, Kindle.

12. Simon N. Young, "Biologic Effects of Mindfulness Meditation: Growing Insights into Neurobiologic Aspects of the Prevention of Depression," *Journal of Psychiatry and Neuroscience : JPN* 36, no. 2

(March 2011): 75–77, https://doi.org/10.1503/jpn.110010.

13. Eric R. Braverman, *Younger Brain, Sharper Mind: A 6-Step Plan for Preserving and Improving Memory and Attention at Any Age from America's Brain Doctor* (New York: Rodale, 2013), loc. 236ff, Kindle.

14. Patty Van Cappellen et al., "Effects of Oxytocin Administration on Spirituality and Emotional Responses to Meditation," *Social Cognitive and Affective Neuroscience* 11, no. 10 (October 1, 2016): 1579–87, https://doi.org/10.1093/scan/nsw078.

15. Friederike Fabritius and Hans W. Hagemann, *The Leading Brain: Powerful Science-Based Strategies for Achieving Peak Performance* (TarcherPerigee, 2017), loc. 2663, Kindle.

16. Bingaman, loc. 239–47, Kindle.

17. Omar Singleton et al., "Change in Brainstem Gray Matter Concentration Following a Mindfulness-Based Intervention Is Correlated with Improvement in Psychological Well-Being," *Frontiers in Human Neuroscience* 8 (February 2014): 33, https://doi.org/10.3389/fnhum.2014.00033.

18. Sharon Begley, *Train Your Mind, Change Your Brain: How a New Science Reveals Our Extraordinary Potential to Transform Ourselves* (New York: Ballantine Books, 2008).

19. Patrick S. Murray and Philip V. Holmes, "An Overview of Brain-Derived Neurotrophic Factor and Implications for Excitotoxic Vulnerability in the Hippocampus," *International Journal of Peptides* 2011 (September 28, 2011): e654085, https://doi.org/10.1155/2011/654085.

20. Rick Hanson, PhD,"Confronting the Negativity Bias," accessed May 17, 2018, www.rickhanson.net/how-your-brain-makes-you-easily-intimidated.

21. Judson A. Brewer et al., "Meditation Experience Is Associated with Differences in Default Mode Network Activity and Connectivity," *Proceedings of the National Academy of Sciences* 108, no. 50 (December 13, 2011): 20254–59, https://doi.org/10.1073/pnas.1112029108.

22. Manoush Zomorodi, *Bored and Brilliant: How Spacing Out Can Unlock Your Most Productive and Creative Self* (New York: St. Martin's Press, 2017), loc. 398, Kindle.

23. Michael I. Posner, Yi-Yuan Tang, and Gary Lynch, "Mechanisms of White Matter Change Induced by Meditation Training," *Frontiers in Psychology* 5 (October 27, 2014), https://doi.org/10.3389/fpsyg.2014.01220.

24. Matt Tenney and Tim Gard, *The Mindfulness Edge: How to Rewire Your Brain for Leadership and Personal Excellence Without Adding to Your Schedule* (Hoboken, NJ: Wiley, 2016), loc. 3158, Kindle.

HOW CAN YOU TELL IF YOU'RE ACTUALLY GROWING?

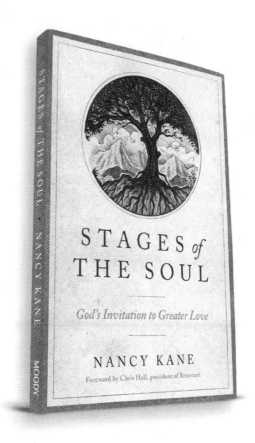

MOODY
Publishers®

From the Word to Life®

Nancy Kane explores the five stages of the soul's journey toward loving God. From stage one, first love, to stage five, intimate love, you will learn where you are, how to grow in love toward God and others, and how to embrace a faith that heals and fills you.

978-0-8024-1690-2 | also available as an eBook